Raising Preschoolers

Also by Dr. Sylvia Rimm

How to Parent So Children Will Learn
Why Bright Kids Get Poor Grades

Raising Preschoolers

Parenting for Today

Dr. Sylvia Rimm

THREE RIVERS PRESS
NEW YORK

Dedicated to Miriam, Benjamin,
Daniel, Rachel, Hannah, and
other grandchildren yet unborn.

~~~~~

Published by Three Rivers Press, New York, New York.
Member of the Crown Publishing Group.

Random House, Inc. New York, Toronto, London, Sydney, Auckland
www.randomhouse.com

THREE RIVERS PRESS is a registered trademark and the
Three Rivers Press colophon is a trademark of Random House, Inc.

Printed in the United States of America

Design by Susan Hood

Library of Congress Cataloging-in-Publication Data
Rimm, Sylvia B.
Raising preschoolers : parenting for today / Sylvia Rimm.
Includes index.
1. Preschool children. 2. Child rearing. 3. Parenting
I. Title.
HQ774.5.R55   1997
649'.123—dc21   97-18764
CIP

ISBN 0-609-80163-5

15 14 13 12 11 10 9 8 7

Acknowledgments

I would like to acknowledge NBC's *Today* show for permitting and assisting me in making the preschool videotape series, which resulted in this book. I'd like to thank Jeff Zucker, executive producer; Janet Schiller, producer of *Raising Kids in the 90's* segments; and Clare Tully, director of development for NBC. I especially appreciate having the opportunity to share questions and discussions about preschool topics with Katie Couric. Katie's parenting experiences and questions made our discussions realistic and fun.

I would also like to thank Steve Ross, editorial director of Crown Publishing, who recognized the value of publishing my book to accompany the NBC videotapes, as well as Ann Patty and Patrick Sheehan for their editorial assistance. Thanks, too, to Harry Trumbore, who captured important family humor in his illustrations.

I have also received considerable assistance from my children and their spouses who deal with the day-to-day parenting issues of preschoolers. My daughter, Sara Rimm-Kaufman, Ph.D., a developmental psychologist, reviewed the entire book and made multiple excellent suggestions, and was especially helpful in her recommendations related to readiness for kindergarten. My daughter-in-law Janet Rimm also reviewed the entire book and contributed considerable invaluable and practical information, particularly as related to nutrition, travel, playdates, and childproofing. My daughter and son-in-law Ilonna and Joseph Madsen and their nanny, Eileen Ihm, contributed the nanny's page from their children's personal journals. My close and loving observations of the skills of all our children and their spouses, Ilonna, Joe, David, Janet, Eric, Allison, Sara, and Alan, in caring for our preschool grandchildren, helped make this book very personal and meaningful.

I would also like to thank all the families of preschoolers who come to my clinic and those who ask me questions—on my radio show as well as through my syndicated newspaper columns and the Internet—for giving me experience with a wide variety of the day-to-day issues parents face when raising their preschoolers.

Special thanks go to Joanne Riedl for her significant editing and proofreading skills. Thanks also to Karen Gary, school psychologist for the Elyria schools; Remae Murdock, experienced preschool teacher; and Elizabeth Greco, mother of two preschoolers—for their helpful insights and suggestions. Thanks go also to Noreen Jocelyn for collecting important information on kindergarten readiness skills for my book. Thanks as always to Marilyn Knackert, Marian Carlson, Karen Ukleja, Alice Poduska, and Terri Vicek for their continuous support.

My appreciation is also extended to my agent, Pierre Lehu, who is always supportive and who so strongly encouraged me to write this book to accompany the NBC videotapes.

Finally, my continuous love and appreciation goes to my husband, the father of our own children, who not only helped me parent them effectively but has also encouraged me to pursue my interests and has never been intimidated by my career, my writing, or my media work, and has also patiently shared vacations with a wife who was enthusiastically writing this book instead of playing.

Contents

Introduction

Parenting preschool children is an awesome responsibility. Children's preschool years are critical for developing cognitive abilities, independence, motor coordination, creativity, and, perhaps most important, positive attitudes toward life. Parents should be loving leaders and teachers for their children. Planning children's preschool years in a positive atmosphere is likely to foster children's love of learning for the rest of their lives.

The suggestions in this book and on the NBC *Today* videotape that complements it will help you guide your children from toddlerhood through kindergarten. Prepare to be patient, and don't expect perfection. Perfect parenting doesn't exist in the real world and is probably not even good for children. The qualities that will help you most as you raise your children are your love for them, enthusiasm, a sense of humor, patience, and the courage to be firm and consistent. Whatever your children's abilities are, if they learn to concentrate, persevere, take initiative, develop interests, and stay positive, they're likely to achieve in school and life and, thus, feel good about themselves.

Of course, your children's achievements are not your only goals. You'll want to teach kindness, sensitivity, responsibility, and assertiveness. You'll also have some special agendas for your children as you look back at your own personal development. You may want to teach skills and provide opportunities you believe you missed when you were a child. There may also be important principles in your own life that you will want to continue. You can probably accomplish much of what you wish for your children if you take time to think about the values that you prefer to cultivate in them. And don't forget, humor and fun are important ingredients in the parenting process.

Most parents feel a little awed at what may be expected of them. Parenting is both a "day at a time" and a long-range goals experience. I hope I can prevent you from feeling overwhelmed by helping you make your children's "day at a time" richer, happier, and more comfortable while also providing a long-term satisfying life for your family.

Raising Preschoolers: Parenting for Today was written for parents, child-care providers, preschool teachers, and grandparents who are caring for children. The accompanying videotape, a presentation with Katie Couric, originated on NBC's *Today* show and includes some of the book's topics. This book can also be used in conjunction with my parenting workbook course, *Parenting for Achievement* (Apple Publishing, 1995), and my book, *Dr. Sylvia Rimm's Smart Parenting* (Crown Publishers, 1996). Of course, it can be used independently of any of these resources.

The chapters in *Raising Preschoolers* are organized by topic; thus, parents can use the book as a reference for finding solutions to a particular problem by consulting either the detailed Contents or the Index, or by reading the entire book. Each chapter includes a description of issues related to the topic, Summary Advice, and specific examples of questions and answers from my syndicated newspaper column, "Sylvia Rimm on Raising Kids." Some of the questions and answers expand on issues discussed in the chapter, while others simply provide concrete examples that parents have asked about. The titles of the questions will help you select the ones most applicable to your family situation.

The foundation of good parenting is team parenting. Whether the members of the team are parents, grandparents, or child-care providers, it's recommended that all of your children's caretakers read this book to encourage communication among the team members. It's important that the whole team be exposed to similar material and that they then take some time to discuss agreements or disagreements they may have with one another about the recommendations in the book. To facilitate better communication, each reader could underline with a different color marker points he or she would like to discuss.

Whether you're reviewing the book alone or together, the Summary Advice in each chapter encapsulates the main recommendations of the chapter. These summary points can lead you to the issues that concern you most and help you target areas to be discussed. The summary can also serve as an important review for approaches you unconsciously repeat. You may even wish to write down some of the critical issues and tape a list to a mirror in a room where you and/or your spouse can't miss it.

The pictures are provided to encourage laughter. Humor helps in raising kids. Enjoy the fun despite the occasional frustrations of parenting your preschoolers.

1

Planning Your Preschooler's Day

The beginning of an infant's life is significant for both the infant and parents, but it is not conducive to planning a schedule. Feeding, changing, bathing, and sleeping fill a twenty-four-hour cycle, and individual temperament differences and physical needs seem to dictate children's daily schedules more than parents' schedules. Mainly, parents use all their energy to feed, nurture, and love their newborn infants. They hope to get sufficient sleep themselves, but usually they feel incredibly tired. Despite parental exhaustion, incredible bonding takes place.

After about three months, most babies' schedules gradually become a little more predictable, and by the toddler and preschool years, parents can begin to arrange for some order and expectation in their children's days and nights. A predictable schedule that allows some flexibility helps children develop healthy habits for eating, sleeping, playing, and learning. It also guides children more positively because it sets expectations. Furthermore, it helps caretakers stay in a more positive, relaxed frame of mind and provides for better communication between caretakers. The caretakers behave more predictably and so do the children. A lack of planning can lead to a chaotic and negative childhood.

While preschool learning and accomplishment is difficult for parents to measure, daily routines teach independence, verbal skills, motor coordination, and, perhaps most important, confidence and love. If parents use scolding and spanking as their main approach to teaching, preschoolers learn negative attitudes about themselves and life. If parents don't plan or organize their children's days, they are also more likely to depend on the negative to limit children's wanderings and explorations. Planning and structure prevent the preschool years from being a battle and permit parents to appreciate the day-to-day progress their children make.

Using a Schedule

When planning your preschooler's days, think about the specific activities in those days; for example, meals, snacks, naps, playing alone, reading, bath, picking up toys, playing with siblings and peers, etc. If you work outside the home, your children's time with child-care providers should be included in your planning, in addition to the time you spend with your children. List the daily activities of each of your preschool children; a sample list follows.

Daily Activities List for Aaron
Breakfast, lunch, evening meal, two snacks
Bath
Nap (approximately two hours)
Bedtime
Plays with Robert (neighbor)
Plays alone indoors
Read to Aaron
Go for walk with Aaron and friend
Listens to musical tapes
Watches *Barney*
Watches *Sesame Street*
Aaron plays with Dad
Pick up toys
Dress

Feel free to make copies of the blank weekly schedule on page 21. You may wish to use self-sticking labels to plan your day: write one activity on each label and move the labels around on the calendar until you have a comfortable schedule. Use your first schedule for initial planning; a second should be used after discussion with your child's other parent and/or child-care provider; and a third should be used after actually applying and evaluating the schedule for several days. You may wish to make additional copies for later use. A sample schedule, filled in, is shown on page 20.

Flexibility

Remember that your schedule is only a guideline. You will need to be flexible and sensitive to your children's daily needs and cues, and you will frequently want to make exceptions. Be sure to leave time for safe exploration and time alone. Alternate quiet time with activity, indoor time with outdoor opportunities (weather permitting). Allow sufficient time for transition between activities; for example, "Five minutes more to play before we clean up" helps children ready themselves for change and prevents parents from always feeling and saying, "We're going to be late."

Consider your children's social needs as well as your own. A play group for a two-year-old may be as helpful for you as for the two-year-old. Stimulating experiences with other parents help moms and dads put their own children's behavior into perspective. Be sure to include time to teach children responsibilities such as picking up their toys and putting their soiled clothes in the hamper. Although you don't need to plan this in your calendar, be sure to leave plenty of time for hugs.

Summary Advice

- Allow for safe exploration and time alone.
- Alternate quiet time with activity.
- Alternate indoor and outdoor time.
- Allow for transition between activities.
- Consider your child's social needs and yours.
- Teach children responsibilities.
- Leave plenty of time for hugs.

Boy Has Hard Time Playing Alone

My four-year-old son has difficulty playing alone. He is our first child and the first grandchild, so he has gotten a lot of attention. How can I encourage some time alone for play?

First and only children have a high risk of becoming dependent upon attention. For some children, this dependence becomes almost like an attention addiction. They've become accustomed to adults attending to them, praising them, and playing with them continuously. These highly social children can actually feel attention deprived when parents leave them to their own devices because they are so unaccustomed to playing alone.

Since your son will be in school soon, it's particularly important that this year be dedicated to teaching him how to be more independent and to facilitate his ability to play alone. He needs that time alone to develop initiative and expand his imagination. Children who are attention addicted easily develop behavior problems in school, where they must share attention with many other children.

Choose a regular time each day in order for him to develop a habit of being alone. Explain to him most positively that this can be his own time, and he can choose his own quiet activities. Also, explain that you plan to use this time for your own personal interests and activities. Show him how a mechanical timer works and explain that the buzzer will signal the end of quiet time for him if he'd like to stop his activities. His first quiet times should be short; ten or fifteen minutes may be sufficient. Gradually expand the time to at least a half hour. He may actually learn to enjoy playing alone and wish to continue even after the timer buzzes. It won't be long before you'll be able to eliminate the timer.

Your son is likely initially to complain of boredom. Don't respond by telling him what to do. He'll initiate his own activities eventually if you ignore his complaints. You don't even have to praise him for his newfound interests. We're hoping that, with time and opportunity, the activities with which he chooses to become involved will become rewarding in themselves. Actually, only children if left on their own often become very good at keeping themselves entertained. They only require opportunity, so insist on providing him with some quality creative quiet time, despite his resistance.

Weekly Schedule

	SUNDAY	MONDAY	TUESDAY	WEDNESDAY	THURSDAY	FRIDAY	SATURDAY
7:30–8:00	→	←	Breakfast	→	→	→	→
8:00–8:30	Play with Mom & Dad	←	Watch	"Barney"		→	Play with Mom & Dad
8:30–9:00	Get dressed	←	Get	dressed	→	→	Get dressed
9:00–9:30		Play at home quietly	↓	Play at park (weather permitting)	↓	Grocery shopping	
9:30–10:00	Snack	Snack		Snack		Snack	Snack
10:00–10:30		TV or computer	Preschool		Preschool		
10:30–11:00	TV or computer		↓	TV or computer	↓	TV or computer	
11:00–11:30	Family activities	Story hour at library	↓	Play at home	↓	Play at home	Family activities
11:30–12:00							
12:00–12:30	Lunch						
12:30–1:00				Read	stories		
1:00–1:30	Nap	Nap	Nap	Nap	Nap	Nap	Nap
1:30–2:00	(X)	(X)	(X)	(X)	(X)	(X)	(X)
2:00–2:30	↑			↑		↑	↑
2:30–3:00	Visit			Snack			
3:00–3:30	grand-	Gymnastics	Play with	→	Computer	Play with	Family
3:30–4:00	parents	class	neighbors	→	class	friends	activities
4:00–4:30	or family	Play at home				↑	
4:30–5:00	activities		↑				
5:00–5:30		Pick up toys					
5:30–6:00		Dinner					
6:00–6:30	Dinner	← Play	with Mom & Dad	→	↑	Dinner	Dinner
6:30–7:00	←	Bath &	snack	→			↑
7:00–7:30	←	Read	stories	→		→	→
7:30–8:00	←	Bedtime	→	→		→	→

Weekly Schedule

	SUNDAY	MONDAY	TUESDAY	WEDNESDAY	THURSDAY	FRIDAY	SATURDAY
7:30–8:00							
8:00–8:30							
8:30–9:00							
9:00–9:30							
9:30–10:00							
10:00–10:30							
10:30–11:00							
11:00–11:30							
11:30–12:00							
12:00–12:30							
12:30–1:00							
1:00–1:30							
1:30–2:00							
2:00–2:30							
2:30–3:00							
3:00–3:30							
3:30–4:00							
4:00–4:30							
4:30–5:00							
5:00–5:30							
5:30–6:00							
6:00–6:30							
6:30–7:00							
7:00–7:30							
7:30–8:00							

Single Mother Has Discipline
Problems with Toddler

I am a single parent raising a twenty-month-old boy. He is a very even-tempered child. He is hard to potty train, butts my head, and has picked up some foul language from day care. I work and go to school part time.

The fun is just beginning. Your little guy is becoming a bit more assertive, but this is normal for an almost two-year-old. His even temper will be helpful. Few children are toilet trained before the age of two, so you may have more success if you wait about six months.

I call the two-year-old age terrific because, although children of this age are usually more assertive, they are a lot better at understanding limits. Try to stay positive and arrange activities so that good things come at the end. For example, if you're trying to teach him to pick up his toys, arrange to have a snack or a story after cleanup time.

If your son's favorite word is *no,* ignore his noes, and gently guide him positively to your expectations. You'll find he'll go along with you most of the time if you don't engage him in battles. Keep your discipline directions clear, brief, and in concrete terms.

He's at an age when you can enjoy a more verbal relationship. Lots of reading to him and answering his "whys" can be fun. The latter can also get tiresome when the questions are more an exercise in getting attention than curiosity. Take time to answer his real questions, and change the subject when the whys get repeated over and over.

Be sure to include some time for yourself with adult friends. You need not feel guilty as long as you've left your son with a trustworthy baby-sitter. A little time away will help you to be more patient and kind when you're with your little guy.

It's harder to be a single parent, but many fine young people come from single-parent homes. Your terrific two-year-old can grow to be a happy and successful adult.

2

Enriching Your Children's Environment

When brain activity is high, parents have a unique
opportunity to foster a love of learning.

Philip H. Abelson,
Engineering and Applied
Sciences Editor, *Science*

N ow that you have scheduled your preschoolers' days, you
can heighten your alertness to the many ways you can enrich
your children's environment during these critical learning
years. Remember that brain activity is high during these years,
and children learn rapidly. Potential for future learning is actually
enhanced by the enrichment you provide. Attitudes are also
learned.

Toys That Teach

It is important for your children to love learning. Specific kinds of play may make a difference in your children's learning potential. Following is a list of toys that provide a variety of learning experiences during the preschool years. Although children may have their favorites, be conscientious in providing familiarity with many kinds of play.

When you select gifts for your preschoolers or for their friends, consider toys that will permit them to enhance a variety of skills. It's better for children to become actively involved with toys, rather than just watch toys or push buttons. Active involvement permits coordination, imagination, and preacademic learning to take place simultaneously.

Play as Learning

Children learn through play—creative and educational toys are their tools. Here is a list of types of toys and some of the main skills learned through their use.

TOYS	SKILLS
Art materials (paints, markers, crayons, scissors, tape, etc.)	Creativity, small muscle coordination, spatial skills
Puppets, dolls, dress-up costumes, masks, etc.	Imagination, role playing, emotional expressiveness
Blocks, puzzles, tangrams, building materials, and dominoes	Imagination, spatial skills, organization, planning, number concepts
Music, tapes, nursery rhymes	Spatial, prereading, rhythm, listening skills, large muscle coordination
Letter and number cards, games, and lotto	Prereading, math, cooperative and competitive skills
Books	Imagination, verbal and attention skills

SOURCE: *Dr. Sylvia Rimm's Smart Parenting: How to Parent So Children Will Learn* by S. B. Rimm (New York: Crown Publishers, 1996).

Gender Stereotypes in Play

Because children learn through play, it's important that preschool learning expands beyond gender stereotypes. For example, only rarely have I observed girls playing with blocks in preschools, although block building may enhance children's spatial skills and could potentially have an effect on girls' math skills. Boys seem to be more attracted to all kinds of building play, but it seems worthwhile to encourage such play for girls as well.

Dress-up play enhances imagination, and it seems more difficult to encourage boys to play dress-up. Doll corners also seem to attract fewer boys, although boys are often willing to play the daddy role. Certainly preschool games of playing house give children opportunities to learn about nurturance because a doll or two are usually considered the babies. Parents and teachers benefit by observing the doll corner from time to time. Don't be surprised to find children repeating your own messages, including your tones of voice.

Arts and crafts, including cutting, coloring, pasting, and painting, need to be especially encouraged for boys, who don't seem to be as easily engaged in these tasks. First-grade boys often have handwriting problems. Their lack of experience with pencils and crayons may be partially to blame, so it certainly makes sense to encourage all children to express themselves in the arts for enjoyment, creative expression, and also for practice that can improve their eye-and-hand coordination.

Parents often worry that their children will become more violent if they play with guns. There is no research evidence that documents that toy guns cause children to be violent. Nevertheless, if you are trying to teach children values that are contrary to violence, it certainly seems logical not to glorify guns and weapons. Despite your concern, you may find your children using a stick or their finger as a gun. There seem to be some behaviors you can't control, so it's probably better to ignore, rather than overreact to them.

Reading, Talking, and Questioning

Reading to children is helpful as soon as children can pay attention briefly (for some children as early as six months). Cloth and thick cardboard books are indestructible. Very young children also enjoy books with texture. Touching soft bunnies and rough sandpaper increases their interest and ability to concentrate. Books that encourage simple motions like clapping or patting fascinate small children, and rhythmic and rhyming verses have special appeal. Children often enjoy hearing books multiple times. Even dozens of readings don't seem to bore them. Eventually children will complete your sentences, fill in missing words, and correct you if you intentionally or unintentionally skip a word.

Although sometimes children question you only to get attention, encourage their questioning and their curiosity. You are enhancing their imagination and initiative. Children who are talked to, sung to, and listened to are more likely to grow in their own verbal ability. Learning to rhyme words will enhance their later reading skills. Listening to children's songs and stories increases both speaking and listening skills. Continuous rote learning with flash cards may cause children to feel pressured and has not been proven to show long-term effectiveness.

Game Playing

Playing board and card games with children has a dual function in enrichment. Children learn number concepts and colors and even enhance spatial abilities when counting in a board game or comparing numbers in a card game like *War*. Learning to count the numbers on dice is also helpful, and they learn to recognize numerals as well. Color recognition can be learned from playing cards and markers in a game like *Candyland*.

Important social skills are also learned from game playing. Taking turns and knowing they can't always be first are rudimentary skills that will help children in preschool and on the playground. Learning about being a good loser and learning not to cheat are often difficult experiences for children. Be sure not to let your children win all the time, or they will not learn those important lessons about competition. Hope that by chance alone they will not lose all the time, either. If the game involves skill, you'll need to give them an advantage and explain to them how and why you've done that. You can help balance the disappointment of losing by having the winner do the cleanup or the loser pick the next game. When kids can learn to laugh at their losses, you'll really be accomplishing an important teaching feat.

Television

Children's television programming and computers also provide important and appropriate enrichment. Programs like *Barney* and *Sesame Street* teach good values and encourage children to participate in singing, learning, and playing. On the other hand, continuous television viewing can result in dependence on entertainment instead of active involvement in play. Although parents are often impressed by preschool children's ability to concentrate on television, dependence on it could actually interfere with their attention to tasks in later years when teachers don't put on colorful and active performances in their classrooms. Furthermore, watching television for hours encourages children to be passive and leaves little time for healthier enrichment.

Violence on television is inappropriate for preschoolers. Children are likely to copy the aggressive behavior. After all, for preschoolers kicking or hitting is easier than talking to solve a problem.

The greatest risk of too much television viewing comes during child care. Some child-care providers don't recognize the importance of their role as teachers and may find the task dull and be happy to wile away their days watching television soap operas or talk shows with preschool children at their sides. Such shows introduce children to inappropriate adult material. If you find your children imitating adult communication styles, it may come from exposure to inappropriate television. Most of adult television is inappropriate for preschoolers, so there's a good chance that if your child-care provider loves to watch daytime television, your child is having a very influential negative experience. Direct and clear communication with your child-care provider may help (see chapter 11), but the only way you may ever know whether the provider is following your guidelines is by your children's telling behavior.

Computers

Computers help children learn. Many preschoolers learn basic math and reading skills by use of the computer. They also become comfortable with technology by using a computer regularly. However, like too much television, too much computer use also has serious drawbacks. Your preschool children should be learning how to interact socially, and interaction with the computer doesn't provide practice for talking to or playing with other children. I have worked with several children who spent many preschool hours fascinated by the computer, and they had significant difficulty adjusting to interaction with other children in preschool, kindergarten, and beyond.

Community Enrichment

Neighborhoods and communities are rich in opportunities for learning through play. A neighborhood walk to the playground or fire station, a walk through woods in the snow, an excursion to the library or bookstore, a visit to a petting zoo or children's museum, or even to a neighbor's garden or farm provides a variety of exciting exposure for your preschool children.

Review your schedule and insert daily, weekly, and monthly enrichment opportunities into your preschoolers' scheduled plans. If it seems to take greater effort to expand your children's environment beyond your own immediate neighborhood, consider involving friends or other adult family members in your plans. That will increase the likelihood of your following through. If you're planning to attend a children's museum with friends, you're less likely to cancel because you feel "tired" that day. Your friends will be counting on you, and of course, so will your children.

Lessons and Classes

Appropriate lessons and classes are likely to be available to your children in your community from approximately age three onward. There are two major categories of classes: physical fitness and specialty learning. If your children are in day care or preschool programs, they may already be involved in programming for both categories and not require further lessons. Playtime at home with you may be more important than outside stimulation.

Physical fitness. The physical fitness needs of preschoolers can best be fulfilled by dance, gymnastics, tumbling, or swimming classes. Playing at the park or playground regularly also qualifies as a fitness activity. Your community may provide some beginning sports fun, but generally, competitive sports should be postponed until school age.

It's important that all the classes are developmentally appropriate. For most preschool children, this is not the time for creating professional gymnasts or ballerinas. This is the time for developing coordination and healthy attitudes toward fitness fun. Classes that are geared toward too much performance for audiences are probably inappropriate. If they require large expenditures for costumes or equipment, they are also probably inappropriate. Expect your children to be doing lots of skipping, galloping, running gracefully, simple tumbling, and balancing exercises. Pretend animals will often be part of the classes; music and rhythm instruments may be included; and learning *left* from *right*, counting, and following directions are also important components.

Specialty learning. Specialty learning includes lessons in music, foreign language, story hours, computers, science fun, and arts and crafts. Although traditional music teachers have recommended postponing musical instrument lessons until age seven or eight, the Suzuki approach used for teaching piano or violin appears to be very effective for teaching preschoolers. Instead of reading notes, children learn by listening to and repeating musical sounds. A parent should realize that the method requires considerable parental involvement. Other musical approaches for preschool children may help them respond to beat, tone, pitch, and note value.

Recent research on teaching music, including keyboard and additional group singing, during the preschool years found that spatial ability was enhanced. Spatial ability is important for learning mathematics later. The research findings could not yet predict whether the early spatial gains would become permanent.

Foreign language lessons during the preschool years typically follow a similar model to Suzuki music lessons. Children learn the language by listening, imitation, singing, and playing. Accents are learned more easily during these years.

Libraries have always provided story hours for preschool children and now bookstores offer them, too. Your children will love story hours. Some require parents to stay and others require them to leave. Either way, you and your children can enjoy the time. Listening to the stories will acquaint you with recent good children's literature, or browsing through libraries and bookstores while waiting can provide some luxurious, relaxed quiet time.

Preschool computer classes should also be fun for children.

Providing them with an early introduction to technology will help them adjust most naturally and comfortably to the technical world surrounding them. Don't be surprised if you find yourself learning some new technology from your small children. What becomes automatic for them may feel awkward and unfamiliar to parents, teachers, or grandparents who did not grow up with computers.

Science fun may involve simple hands-on experiments or nature walks and exploration. Learning about plants, animals, shells, rocks, and stars seems to make for natural fun for preschoolers. Science often blends with the arts at this age, so leaf prints and pictures of animals may be incorporated into science classes.

Arts and crafts classes, often taught by community recreation centers and art museums, should emphasize creative expression, but children also benefit from learning the fine muscle coordination skills that will be so helpful in their later schoolwork.

Avoiding Overprogramming

Although preschoolers benefit from lessons, be sure not to overprogram your children. Two or three activities a week suffice. Preschoolers should have plenty of time for play at home. They require rest and time alone with a parent or day-care provider. Continuous activities lead to constant hurrying and pressure instead of wholesome learning. Parents should also consider their own time constraints and pressures in planning for their children.

Summary Advice

- Use toys to teach skills.
- Read, talk to, and answer your children's questions.
- Play games for fun and learning.
- Use television and computers in moderation.
- Consider lessons at around age three.
- Explore your neighborhood and community for rich learning experiences.
- Don't overprogram your children.

Giggles and Jokes During Learning Sessions

My question is about our five-year-old son. He's going into kinder-garten this fall, and when my wife and I work with him at home re-garding numbers or letters, he starts to laugh and giggle and just lose control. He'll think it's all kind of a joke and just funny stuff. What should we do about that? He won't do that in preschool or with other people, but he'll just start giggling when we work with him.

It is good for you and your wife to do a little work with your five-year-old as he'll soon be entering kindergarten. It is also a good sign that he doesn't respond with silliness in preschool. His silly response to you and his mother may be related to anxiety he feels when he works with you.

Plan a regular work time with him for a very short period, less than five minutes at first. Be sure only one adult is with him in the room. Until he feels more comfortable with his work time, do number or letter games, follow the dots, coloring, or cut and paste. Rhymes and poems also make learning more interesting. Praise him for being a hard worker during the very first minute, and re-member, keep the lessons brief. When you're finished, tell your spouse, within your son's hearing, that he seems to be learning well (referential praise). Be sure not to do too much at once or expect him to learn too quickly. Stop working before he's ready to stop. When he asks for more, tell him he must wait until the next day be-cause you are too busy. As he asks for more, extend the time grad-ually. Soon he'll be begging you for more of your precious time and valuing the time you're willing to spend with him.

Children are very sensitive to the anxiety a parent feels in teach-ing them, and your son may feel your teaching as pressure. He may be afraid he can't please you. Shortening the time and selecting fun activities will likely have the effect of lifting the pressure.

If that approach doesn't work, skip a few weeks of work time. Continue reading and playing with him. Try again after a few more weeks. Your son's small muscle coordination may be a bit delayed, which seems to happen with many children, but more with boys than girls. Give him a little more time to get ready. When he's feel-ing ready, he'll stop the silliness and begin enjoying the learning process.

Coping with the Extraordinarily Gifted

Shortly before my daughter's first birthday, I walked into her room one day to check on her during a nap. She was holding a book and was very intently gazing at the pages. When I attempted to take the book away, she said, "No, Mama, words!" Well, that was almost two years ago, and since then, she and I have been many places.

I started out at a pace she would be able to cope with, but it's me who has exceeded the coping. In the past two years, I have read my daughter everything from the Webster's Dictionary *to college-level calculus (I don't understand it). She always says, "Read it again!" She can remember what I'm saying, and I believe she can actually read.*

For a few days I tried not reading to her. She became uncontrollable, stuttered, and wet the bed, so we went back to books. Some days, she's a normal three-year-old, and other days she's like a little sponge soaking up everything. Recently, she walked into the kitchen babbling something about inert gases.

I need to know if I'm doing this right. I can't get her into the school system because there are no programs for children like her. So, we are converting an extra room into a "learning lab."

Just to give you an idea of her favorite subjects, here are a few of the books we've read: Plato's Five Great Dialogues, Knights of the Round Table, Summer Sonnets, Stegosaurus Solar-Powered Dinosaur, *and* World Book Encyclopedia, A–Z. *Help!*

Your three-year-old daughter's interest in books and reading is extraordinary. It is certainly not surprising that you feel befuddled. It is difficult to say from your description whether her high interest and her unique memory will develop into equally high thinking skills, but the characteristics you describe are usually indicators of extreme intellectual giftedness. You do have a challenge ahead, and schools are not likely to be prepared to provide your child with an appropriate challenge.

While you will certainly want to continue to enhance and encourage your daughter's learning, a specific room to be used as a learning laboratory may only serve to narrow your daughter's learning experience to books and equipment. The world, both indoors and outdoors, is probably more appropriate as a laboratory and considerably less limiting. Her thirst for knowledge can be broadened more effectively if she does not connect learning with the confines of books or rooms, although certainly books and equipment will be integral parts of her exploration.

Your greatest challenge will be to encourage her learning without permitting that passion to dominate your family life. Equally critical will be to avoid making her unusual talent the basis for public display or exhibition.

An evaluation by a school psychologist in order to enter her in school a year early is appropriate. A play group or nursery school would be helpful for her now so that she may learn to enjoy the company of age-mates. There are likely to be both challenges and special joys ahead.

Mother Wants Ideas for Enriching Home Environment

Can you make some suggestions for enriching my child's preschool environment at home, in addition to reading to her?

Your home provides your child's first learning experiences. Kitchen science and cooking are equally effective teaching tools. Play-Doh, watercolors, sandboxes, and clay permit your child's creative exploration of the arts. A friendly piano or guitar being played by an amateur musician-parent can become the basis for sing-alongs, dance-alongs, and play-alongs for your daughter. Stores abound with tapes. Hearing taped stories (without visuals) encourages children's listening skills. Dancing to recorded music facilitates children's coordination and love of music. When you join in the dance, your family will become less inhibited and feel even freer. Add some ballet slippers to your dance performances and you'll all even feel graceful.

Be sure to explore your community resources. Art museums, parks, conservatories, museums of natural history or science, aquariums, observatories, nature centers, libraries, children's museums, children's theaters, bookstores, and concert halls may be closer than you realize, and young children can appreciate all of these.

History can come alive to a preschooler with a visit to a grandparent's home or to a home for senior citizens. When seniors tell about their own childhood, it is especially interesting to children. Use a tape recorder to preserve these stories. Old photographs of the young children's senior friends in times gone by enhance these types of experiences for preschool children.

There may be the risk of overwhelming your daughter with too much culture. If you're enthusiastic and she's uninterested, it may be a signal for you either to slow down or do some adult activities without her. Modeling a love of learning provides a most important opportunity for your daughter.

Parents Differ on Enrichment

My husband and I disagree about how we should be challenging our bright three-year-old son. My husband wants to teach him Spanish and buy a computer, and I want to sit on the floor with him and work puzzles and play games. We're not sure what is appropriate.

Your little three-year-old can sit on the floor with you and work puzzles and do games. He can also begin to learn the computer and Spanish from his dad. However, all these activities need to be provided in moderation and without pressure. He needs time to explore, to laugh, to play imaginatively and actively, to dance and enjoy music, and to be read to and talked to. Foster your son's interests as you expose him to learning, and be sensitive to the signs that say he's had enough.

It's too easy to place too much attention on a bright child's knowledge and learning. The result may be that he only feels valued when he's giving correct answers. Your son needs to know that his mom and dad love him not just for his intelligence and that having fun in your family, valuing kindness, and caring about one another are important learning activities as well.

Neither you nor your husband are wrong. Children thrive on challenge, but they suffer when pushed. Be sensitive to your son's readiness as you introduce him to the love of learning.

Problem with Pronunciation

My daughter just turned two years old, and I am concerned about her speech. Although she can say a number of words, she can't pronounce them correctly. She leaves off the first letter of words, and she can't pronounce L, Ch, or Sh. She also confuses her Bs with Ms.

She has just recently started putting two or three of her "words" into sentences.

I have had her tested and everything was normal, but it was suggested that she come back in six months for a follow-up. It becomes quite frustrating at times to interpret what she is trying to say. She has an older brother who is four years old, and his vocabulary at that age was very different. He was speaking in full sentences at eighteen months. Could you advise me on whether speech therapy is needed and how old she should be if it is necessary?

Your daughter, who speaks quite well for a two-year-old, suffers only by the comparison to your verbally capable son. Having difficulty with pronouncing particular sounds is common at age two, and it is only your first experience with your son that causes you to believe there is a problem. Of course, it's frustrating for you not to be able to always understand your two-year-old. That problem may already have improved by the time you read this response, but if it hasn't, it should not be a worry. Some speech problems are common even in kindergarten. However, since the speech therapist suggested a six-month checkup, following her advice is safe. Be assured that most two-year-olds have difficulty pronouncing some sounds.

3

Social-Emotional Learning

Most everyone would agree that teaching children social skills and emotional appropriateness is an important priority and sets the stage for a mentally healthy and happier life ahead. Children are born with different temperaments and, perhaps, even different degrees of emotional intelligence. However, they learn attitudes, interactive skills, and values during their preschool years. Children benefit for the rest of their lives when they are intentionally taught good social skills and values.

Values

Parents teach children values during their entire childhood, but those taught during the preschool years are the foundation for the teaching ahead. Parents have the greatest influence during children's early years. Schools, peers, and the media dramatically affect values during the school-age years. If children are given a good foundation early, they are less likely to be mislead later. The roots of your children's conscience are taught in these early years.

Preschoolers learn values best by stories. They love to listen to stories. *The Boy Who Cried Wolf* has been used millions of times over to teach small children about honesty. Many children's stories are expressly written to convey values. As you read to your children, ask them questions that elicit their thinking about the values they hear. For example, "What would have happened to the little boy's sheep if he hadn't lied the first time?"

Young children love to hear stories about their parents' childhood. There are probably stories you could share about how you learned to be honest, kind, or brave. There may be less favorable stories you remember as well. Don't brag about the times you got in trouble with your parents or teachers unless you can point out a lesson that you learned. If you brag about your troublemaking times, your children can be expected to try to outdo you, but the shoes will be on different feet, and you may not appreciate the naughtiness you've taught your children.

Your children will also be learning values by watching you. If you keep the extra change when the cashier gives you too much, if you brag about cheating on your income taxes, if you're disrespectful to your spouse or parent, you children will literally copy your actions. Look for teaching moments with your children. Tell them that you've given the correct change back, although you could have kept it, because it's important to be fair and honest. Explain that you pay taxes honestly because it's everyone's responsibility to support our government, and you're willing to do your share (although no one is anxious to pay high taxes). Explain that you may have differences with your spouse or mother, but that you're willing to discuss and compromise with the people you love. Life is an exciting story to preschoolers. They don't yet refer to parents' discussions as lectures. They love to listen to you and feel your undivided attention. You have wonderful opportunities to teach good values and to help children distinguish between right and wrong. Remember, preschoolers are very literal and concrete in their thinking. The nuances and ambiguities may need to wait until they're a little older. Preschoolers see and hear you in black and white. The grays and shadings can be postponed for their readiness.

Kindness and Consideration

Children can be taught to be kind and considerate by observing their parents' and caretakers' kindness, by specific explanation of kind behaviors, and by adults valuing, noticing, and praising children's kind behaviors. They can also learn about kindness when parents read or tell stories about kindness or comment on the kindness of others in their environment. For example, when your children carry a kitty that has strayed back to its mommy or help their baby sister or brother pick up their toys, parents can label the behavior as "kind" and tell their children how pleased they are to see that kindness.

There are many books and stories about kindness, and your children will love them. I remember reading a book called *Kindness Is a Lot of Things!* to our children hundreds of times. Following are some excerpts from that book that they have never forgotten. Consider that by teaching your own children to be kind, you are helping to create a kinder and gentler world.

From Kindness Is A Lot of Things!

Kindness is telling a friend that you like him.

Kindness is remembering when it is time for Kitty's dinner.

Kindness is helping someone who can't do something as well as you.

It is sharing your candy and letting someone else have the biggest piece.

Kindness is letting Little Brother help, even when the job would be easier to do yourself.

It is making someone small feel big!

Kindness is helping to pick up around the house.

It is sharing. It is being thoughtful. It is being friendly!

Kindness is a way of showing love!

SOURCE: *Kindness Is A Lot of Things!* by E. Eckblad (C. R. Gibson Company, Norwalk, Connecticut: 1965).

Manners

Manners are only an extension and application of kindness. Your children can learn the magic words *please* and *thank you* soon after they're a year old. The words may sound like "peas" and "ta ta," but they represent important learning. Your children will love the words and so will you. They truly seem like magic words. They define your children as refined and considerate, and open doors to more positive child and adult relationships. Your children's learning will require a fair amount of repetition from you, but it's worth your effort.

Around age two, children can learn to wash their little hands before eating (for health as well as manners), and soon afterward, will be able to ask to have food passed or to be excused from the table. They can even learn to say a polite "No, thank you" instead of "Yuk," even if they don't like broccoli.

Around age three, children are able to ask for permission to use friends' toys, go out to play, have a snack, or invite friends to their home. They're able to clear their place after a meal and push their chairs in at the table.

Around age four, children can learn to answer the telephone politely with, for example, "Hello, I'm David Sparks. Would you like to speak to my daddy?" You can teach them how to answer the phone by role-playing with them on a toy telephone. They're able to leave a message on your answering machine or give you a message like, "Mommy, Mr. Major would like to talk to you. He's at the front door."

To accomplish these lovely manners, you are required only to teach them the words and behaviors to use. Children will then begin to use them automatically. Friends and neighbors will praise your children's refinement, and the behaviors will be reinforced permanently. What a pleasure your kids will be to all! They'll smile a lot, and their social confidence will grow. When the negative playground language they hear interferes with the language you've taught them, you'll only need to remind them that they have much better language to use. Teachers will love your kids and other nice kids will, too. The kids with atrocious manners who push and shove and grab will either keep their distance or learn some nice manners from your children.

Expressing Feelings and Developing Sensitivity

Preschool children don't always feel kind. Sometimes they feel angry, sad, or worried. They need the opportunity to express their feelings in words and sometimes in tears. They don't always understand their own feelings, which complicates matters. Although parents can walk away from or time-out children's temper tantrums (see chapter 8), they should listen to kids when they express their frustration or anger in words. Parents can even say to them, "You can tell me when you're angry and you can tell me why you're angry. I may not be able to change what you'd like me to change, but I can at least hear about your feelings."

Probably the best way children can learn how to express feelings appropriately is by listening to parents express their feelings to them. When a friend or family member gets sick or dies, help children understand your sadness. If you feel especially stressed, you can explain that simply. If you're worried about your job or that of a friend, you can share your anxiety. Although children need the security of knowing you can continue on despite your sadness, hiding your feelings will only prevent their knowing that you're feeling anything.

There is a fine line between expressing feelings and overprotecting; for example, some children become anxious over a new experience. Parents who feel worried about the child's anxiety sometimes make too big an issue of the child's anxious feelings in order to protect him. Instead of getting over their anxiety, the child seems to become more anxious. It probably would be better to make no comment or simply to reassure the child that the anxiety will disappear once he's involved in the activity.

Although preschoolers don't have much insight about the causes of the feelings they have, children develop sensitivity and insight by being encouraged to talk about their feelings and by you listening to them. They are encouraged to express feelings only if you take time from your busy day to hear about their problems and sensitivities. They also learn to be sensitive by hearing your sensitive interpretation of events. Here's an example of how parents can develop sensitivity in their children or, alternatively, how they can destroy sensitivity:

A family is watching the news together, and although Carlie is playing a game on the other side of the room, she stops her play and joins her parents when the TV screen fills with sad and starving children. The questions follow quickly: Why are they hungry? Where are their parents? Why don't they have clothes? Why aren't they playing?

A response that would help Carlie understand how sad the circumstances are and how troubled these children are will increase her sensitivity. A suggestion of sending a small contribution will teach her the beginning of social responsibility. A response that would ignore her feelings or the feelings of the children on the television would suggest a lack of empathy and desensitize her to the problems of others.

Me Firsters and Poor Losers

Preschoolers are by definition self-centered. Wanting to be first, to have more than their siblings, and never to lose a game are all natural and not symptomatic of problems, as they might be at age nine or ten. Those behaviors all provide opportunities to teach sharing, taking turns, and being a good sport. You'll want to repeat your lessons multiple times and praise your kids for being patient, good sharers, and fair players.

While some game playing is appropriate so they can learn to win and lose, too much competition will be hard for children to cope with during these early years. Don't expect them to be soccer stars or beauty queens, or they will internalize impossible pressures. Children may seem to enjoy all the attention at the time, but they will feel rejected and neglected if the talent or beauty doesn't continue.

Chasing, Roughhousing, and Tickling

Chasing, roughhousing, and tickling are typical expressions of love between parents and preschoolers. Closeness, mirth, and laughter are the fun by-products. Even in this area, children must learn to accept limits.

Parents of toddlers often ask me why their children run away when they call them to come in from play. I ask the parents if they play "chase" with their children, and the response is most always yes. Toddlers sometimes have trouble differentiating your serious call from the chasing game, and the game is just more fun. If it doesn't cause any problem for you, play "chase" all you like. However, if the chasing is frustrating you and giving mixed signals to your child, suspend the game temporarily.

The same holds true for tickling and roughhousing. When you observe your kids in trouble because they tickled, hit, or wrestled too much with other kids, stop those activities at home for at least a little while, and they will, too. You can reintroduce the family fun if your children's behavior improves on the playground with peers.

Chores and Responsibilities

Children should begin to learn responsibilities around age two, although you will probably have to work alongside them with each new responsibility. They should be able to pick up their toys, put their soiled clothes in the hamper, and clear their dishes from the table. They may also hang up their coats on a hook and place their boots or shoes neatly in a closet. They may be able to retrieve the newspaper or mail (depending on location of the boxes). Around age three, they should be able to help you set the table and assist in making their beds.

You can help your children learn to be responsible by talking about and demonstrating your own responsibilities. For example, you could say, "Before we leave, I have to clean up the kitchen counter just as you have to pick up your toys."

Children this age are wonderful "gofers." They love to go on brief errands to other rooms to find something you may need, and they appreciate the thank-yous for their help. They feel so valued. They can help find ingredients in a low cupboard if you're cooking and can bring safe tools to you if you're involved in a carpentry project. They grow in confidence as you praise them as good helpers.

If you have a pet, your preschoolers can help by holding the bowl while you fill it for feeding. They can also accompany you while you walk the dog and perhaps hold the leash for a little while, depending, of course, on the dog's temperament. If you have a garden, they can help you to plant seeds and even help you pull a few weeds.

You may want to construct a picture chart for each of your children's daily chores. Each evening before bedtime you can place a star on the chart for each of the chores they completed that day. No prizes or gifts are necessary. The stars are enough to make them feel proud of their accomplishments. Praising them as good helpers also builds their confidence.

Helping Children Learn About Their Bodies

The first lesson in simple sexuality given to preschoolers is the identification of body parts. You'll want to add to eyes, ears, and hands, the body parts like vulva, penis, buttocks, and breasts. If you prefer to use shortcut names, like "wee wee" or "butt," it will probably do no harm, but the use of correct terms from the start may eliminate some later tension for children because the words will seem natural. Hopefully, when a neighbor arrives, your children will not embarrass you with a comment like, "Look at Mrs. Jones's big breasts," even though Mrs. Jones would undoubtedly laugh in understanding.

Questions about the birth of babies usually arise if you or a neighbor is expecting a baby. Although preschoolers are curious, they require only brief answers. You won't have to tell them all about sex at this time (see chapter 12).

Preschoolers are so delightfully uninhibited and comfortable with their bodies that they're often happy to run through the house unclothed and laughing. They'll even say things such as "I like to be naked, do you?" Yet by the time they enter preschool, they will need to cover their bodies when others are around and, without causing any harm, will require some lessons to protect their bodies.

Private parts should be labeled as private, and even four-year-olds should learn about good touching and bad touching. If they're not sure about a family member's or other child's touching, they should be encouraged to report the touching to Mom or Dad. You can then reassure children about appropriate hugs and investigate any suspicious touching.

Preschoolers are normally curious about one another, so, for the most part, parents don't need to be concerned about other preschoolers investigating each other, particularly if children have not seen children of the opposite gender without diapers or clothes on. They're simply curious. It's important not to overreact to normal preschool interest. Heightened consciousness about reporting sexual abuse has sometimes led to overreaction or overreporting by adults. Protective attitudes about children's bodies should be preserved, but positive, healthy attitudes toward sexuality should also be encouraged.

If your child is acting flirtatious or sexual, it's worthwhile to investigate the cause. Preschoolers certainly don't have any understanding of what they're behaviors are communicating, and are probably copying them. It's best simply to say that the inappropriate behaviors are just "not nice" for a little girl or boy. Children don't need further explanation, but you may certainly want to understand the cause of the behaviors. Magazine pictures or television may be their teachers, but also check up on baby-sitters, teens in the neighborhood, inappropriate dance or modeling classes, or relatives who may think the behaviors are cute. Sexual children are vulnerable to sick adults in and out of the family.

Humor

Humor is an important part of children's social-emotional learning. Parents often joke with children and tease in a good-humored way, which can help children understand that joking is acceptable and fun. Sometimes humor can be used to distract children from their anger or their wish to have something immediately. It's most fun when children begin to try to make up their own jokes. Well, actually it's difficult sometimes to tell what the joke is about, and other times parents simply get tired of hearing the same joke over and over. Children do tend to repeat jokes frequently and often giggle as they tell them and for a long time afterward. Considering that a sense of humor is helpful in moving through life, perhaps it's worth encouraging—or at least surviving—the corniness. On page 45 is a group of jokes by three- to six-year-olds. Do encourage laughter in your children. It's healthy even when it gets a little silly.

Examples of Preschool Humor

Q: Why was six afraid of seven?
A: Because seven ate (eight) nine.

Q: What did one volcano say to the other volcano?
A: I lava you.

Mom: Your daddy went to Toronto.
Child: He went to torontosaurus?

Q: Why did the turtle take a ladder to school?
A: Because he wanted to go to high school.

Q: Why did the chicken cross the playground?
A: To get to the other slide.

Child: Where do cows go on Friday nights?
Mom: I give up. Where?
Child: To the moooovies!

Child: Grandma, will you remember me in a day?
Grandma: Yes.
Child: Will you remember me in a week? In two weeks? In three weeks?
Grandma: Yes (to all those questions).
Child: Knock, knock.
Grandma: Who's there?
Child: Grandma, did you forget me already?

Play Groups

If you are at home with your children full time, a play group where they can learn to interact with a few other children and learn to share attention is a high priority. It is a reasonable social priority for your own interactions with other parents as well. It's best to keep play groups small during the preschool years. Even numbers of children work better than odd numbers; four to six children might be ideal, and even as few as two will provide simple social interaction. Children's play may only be side by side rather than interactive at first. Interactive play can include informal, sponta-neous play, simple art projects, stories, music, and action games.

Playdates

By the time your children are ages three or four, play groups may evolve to playdates, an arrangement whereby your child either visits a friend's home or a friend visits your home. With the complicated schedules of most families, even children's social lives require planning. Sometimes arrangements may need to be made several days or a week in advance. Parents may wish to make arrangements outside of children's hearing to avoid the disappointment that comes with postponements because of busy schedules. If you and/or your spouse are working outside the home, your nanny or child-care provider may be planning these social events. However, as parents, you should be sure some (and not too many) of these events are happening. Research shows that these experiences will help your children initiate social contacts when they enter school.

Playdates provide a great opportunity for kids to develop social skills, have special time with a friend, and play with other kids' toys. They also provide a chance for parents to see their children in different roles. Two to three hours may be the best starting length of time for a playdate so they can end while everyone is still happy. You may want to make first playdates as short as an hour to help children adjust.

As a parent hosting a playdate, you have the unique opportunity to do some unobtrusive listening and observing. Although you want to be careful to give children time and space together, you can nevertheless notice the way your own child interacts with another child. While you're folding the laundry or unloading the dishwasher, you can tell if your child is assertive enough or too aggressive. You can notice whether your child shares, compromises, and initiates activities. If she seems bossy, you may use this opportunity to teach leadership. If she's hesitant, you can teach assertiveness. Sometimes you can intervene for social teaching opportunities, but mostly, you can collect information for teaching your child social skills at another time and place.

If there are other close-age siblings, it's a good idea to make a plan for the other children as well. They can have a friend visit or go to a different friend's home. Sometimes you can have some special one-to-one time with a sibling while permitting the other child to play with her friend alone. Although from time to time siblings may join in, for the most part playdates are intended to give your children friendship experiences without siblings.

It's a good idea for parents to alternate hosting and visiting so children may experience both roles (and toys!). Because most kids want a snack, parents should clarify any potential food issues before the playdate, including food sensitivities (lactose intolerance, food allergies) or if the child eats a special diet—only kosher foods, a vegetarian diet, or primarily peanut butter and jelly, for example.

While the focus of a playdate should be having fun together, it may be helpful to review a few expectations you have of your children prior to playdates to avoid later conflicts: Can doors be closed or must they remain open? Do you allow TV or movies? How do you handle cleanup? Putting away toys/cleanup should be part of every playdate. It's probably best with parent(s) helping. With just a little simple communication, playdates can provide excellent social learning for your children.

Birthday Parties

Preschoolers' birthday parties are special, although sometimes they can get out of control. They may include a family, school, and friends party—and that may be more socialization and more gifts than any three- or four-year-old can handle. The problem of size is frequently related to not wanting to hurt other children's feelings, and, of course, that's logical and considerate. Although a small party of three to six children is probably more appropriate and more manageable for a preschooler, it's worthwhile inviting a few extra children to teach your child to be considerate of the feelings of others and not leave children out.

Parents can have considerable creative fun in planning parties with playful themes. A theme approach can provide interesting learning experiences for your preschoolers as well as encourage their imagination as they explore these themes. If party favors are given to all the guests, be sure the birthday boy or girl gets one, too. It is, after all, his or her special day.

Parents are usually included in parties of children up to age three, which helps the children feel more secure. By age four, children are often dropped off at parties, which makes them feel more independent. To keep the party manageable, it's probably best to keep it fairly brief. Be ready for juice to spill and at least one child to cry. Preschoolers are, after all, only learning social skills. Your camera will preserve those golden moments forever, so despite the number of minor disasters, don't lose the opportunity to have at least one birthday party a year for each of your children.

Summary Advice

- Teach preschoolers kindness and manners.
- Encourage children to express their feelings.
- Help children cope with competition.
- Notice the effects of roughhousing and chasing.
- Build confidence with chores and responsibilities.
- Help children be comfortable with their bodies.
- Encourage humor.
- Include cleanup as a part of every playdate.
- Set up play groups and playdates for opportunities for social interaction and observation.
- Provide birthday parties for special social interactions.

Young Perfectionist

I have two sons, ages four and one, and I have a concern about my oldest son. During my conference with his preschool teacher, she told me that when he begins a project at school, he becomes very frustrated and says he "can't do it." He just comes "unglued." I get the impression that if he can't do something perfectly, he doesn't want to even try, and I'm very upset over his attitude. I try to explain to him that his baby brother, who is just learning to walk, keeps falling down, but he keeps getting up and trying again.

My husband and I are very supportive of him and not negative people. We are always encouraging him. My husband thinks I am overreacting to this situation, but I don't think I am. Is there any way we can help him? I want him to have a good start at school.

You and your husband are both right. Since a preschool teacher has shared her concern about your son's attitude, you can assume that the problem is real and not an overreaction. Your husband's perception is also correct, as your anxiety may be complicating the problem for your son.

Your child is exhibiting early signs of perfectionism, which can sometimes lead to underachievement. Firstborn children, particularly if they are very verbal, often get extreme praise and attention from adults. They may internalize the praise as messages of expectation. As preschoolers, it rarely causes them a problem, but since you now have another child, your son may be feeling the "dethronement" or sibling rivalry that often becomes more obvious when the second child becomes a toddler.

Your son's frustration with his imperfection seems to be garnering attention in school and causing extreme anxiety at home. When children become anxious about their performance, too much discussion about the problem seems to become an unconscious power struggle. The more the parent reassures, the more reassurance the child seems to require and the less confidence he seems to develop. Your comments about mistakes and efforts are appropriate, but try not to belabor them. A one-sentence, matter-of-fact statement will be sufficient. Be moderate in the praise of your son's accomplishments. That's a "nice" picture instead of a "spectacular" or "magnificent" picture will tell him you're pleased with his drawing without putting pressure on him. Also use moderate praise for perseverance, learning from his mistakes, and putting effort into projects.

You've made mention of how positive and encouraging you and your husband are with your son. In general, that's very good parenting. However, sometimes it can lead to overpraise, which becomes "too much of a good thing" and causes even preschool children to believe parents expect too much of them. Firstborn children are particularly vulnerable to that problem.

You can have high hopes that your son will not be an underachiever because you have identified the problem early enough to keep it from becoming more serious.

Girl Puts Dresses on Little Brother

I have a five-year-old daughter and a three-year-old son. They play together all the time. Both are very imaginative and like to dress up. The problem is that my daughter dresses my son in dresses, and they have fun doing it. How can I make sure that they are clear about gender roles?

Playing dress-up often involves clothes of either gender, but boys tend to do more of the cross-gender dressing than girls, mainly because the play-clothes collection usually includes more of Mom's old clothes than Dad's. Add a supply of Dad's pants and old shirts and a fireman or police hat, and they'll soon be dressing in a variety of gender clothes.

If seeing your son in dresses really bothers you, ask your daughter not to put dresses on him. Simply explain that girls wear dresses and pants, but boys never wear dresses. If you're firm, she'll get the idea, and you'll feel more relaxed. However, the change is only necessary for your peace of mind rather than for any fear of gender confusion.

Boy Likes to Play with Barbie Dolls

Is there such a thing as gender-appropriate toys? I have a three-and-a-half-year-old son who, when given a choice, tends to choose toys that we would associate with girls, such as Barbie dolls. This is a concern to my husband because he had a brother who was gay. He's uncomfortable about it. Should we be discouraging this?

Preschool- and kindergarten-age children often choose toys that can be associated with both genders. Dress-up clothes, either male or female outfits, are fun for all children and encourage their imaginative play.

Barbie dolls are not truly appropriate for preschoolers, boy or girl. Baby or child dolls of both genders are more appropriate. A boy doll would probably also cause your husband to feel more comfortable.

By first or second grade, boys tend to be more gender selective, but even then it would not be unusual for a boy or girl to play dress-up. It would be more unusual for a boy to become overinvolved with Barbie dolls, except in the role of brother or dad or Ken.

In an era when both males and females become involved in both child care and careers, it seems psychologically healthy for children to play with the whole continuum of toys rather than only those that are sex-role stereotyped.

Your husband's expression of his anxiety is better than pretending he isn't worried. Building a good father-son relationship is good for boys, regardless of what their sexual orientation becomes in adulthood. If your husband and son spend lots of time together doing work in and around the house, enjoying sports, or just doing errands, your son is likely to feel comfortable with his own masculinity. It's important, too, that you, as the mom, don't become the mediator of that relationship. In other words, if you keep telling your husband how to act with your son, he will soon tire of being advised.

If your son is accustomed to being a "mama's boy"—and that is not unusual for a three-and-a-half-year-old—when he asks to stay home with you instead of going with his dad, assure him that you are busy and that his dad requires his help. If you don't play the role of shelterer, they'll soon find each other. If you withdraw a little from their special relationship, male bonding and camaraderie will just occur.

Mainly, I'm hoping that neither Mom nor Grandmom nor Dad are truly worried. Cross-gender play at this age is not a predictor of homosexuality. However, if either of these little boys do grow up to choose a homosexual way of life, I am hoping that Mom, Grandmom, and Dad will continue to love them and respect their choices.

4

Discipline

Parents and teachers are concerned about appropriate discipline for their kids from the time they are toddlers through middle childhood and the teenage years. The goal of discipline is to lead children toward values and learning skills that will prepare them for adulthood, when they will eventually depend entirely on self-discipline. The hope is that their personal discipline will result in happy, fulfilling, and caring lives.

Your pleasure in your children's accomplishments and your disappointment in their inappropriate behaviors are your most effective tools when disciplining your children. Realistic parents also find that there are times when raising their voices slightly or setting firm limits are the requirements for helping their children grow in confidence. There should always be a positive emphasis in your disciplinary techniques.

When and how to discipline varies considerably according to

both developmental stage and individual temperament. Although your family values will shape the direction of your children's growth, genetic makeup at birth determines a child's temperament, levels of energy, and capabilities. Of course, school, peer, and even sibling environments will also affect your children's discipline requirements as they mature. There are, however, some discipline generalizations that seem to fit all ages and personalities. Your first priority is to teach your children positively; your second is to set limits firmly if your children have temporarily gone astray.

Discipline begins as soon as babies can crawl or toddle. Making spaces child-safe by rearranging, locking, or protecting is much more effective than slapping hands and saying "no" every few minutes. Of course, no environment can be completely childproof. Saying "no" or a descriptive word, such as "hot," in a slightly raised and serious voice, paired with a distraction to some other toy or activity, work well until children approach two years of age. Biting or hitting can be retaught with a "no" followed by a "nice" while giving a patting or hugging lesson. When that is ineffective, a brief time-out in a crib or room will usually work (see chapter 8).

The Important Relationship Between Discipline and Freedom

Discipline and freedom are inextricably connected. Your approach to disciplining your children will make a difference in how freely they feel and act. Unlike the "day at a time" daily routines you planned in the first chapter, it's important when planning a disciplinary philosophy to view your children's full life span. If you are rigid too early, you may be teaching your child to be too fearful and inhibited as an adolescent and adult. If you are too negative and punishing, you will teach your child to be angry and aggressive. If you permit too much freedom, you could be fostering impulsiveness or promiscuity by the teenage years. If children are allowed adult decision making early, they won't have the wisdom to make those decisions and will expect to be allowed to make them later. If you permit too much freedom early and want to pull in the reins later because your children have gone beyond what you believe is safe, you will create a very rebellious adolescent. Following are some case study examples.

Obedience Gone Awry

Rodney was Mike and Andrea's first child. Both Mike and Andrea were therapists who specialized in working with dysfunctional, out-of-control adolescents. The parents were both determined that they would bring up a disciplined son who would not behave in the manner they observed in teenagers they worked with. They wanted to prove they could teach their son to be obedient early on.

They decided that instead of childproofing their home or using gates, they would teach Rodney by saying "no" firmly and spanking his hand hard each time he touched a plant or knob that he shouldn't touch. They were very consistent and determined, and Rodney soon learned limits that were almost everywhere for him. He was actually unusually obedient.

By age four, when I evaluated Rodney, he was a timid, fearful child who took little initiative. His preschool was concerned about his shyness and lack of participation and even questioned the possibility of depression. He got into absolutely no trouble, but had so little confidence in himself that he feared participation in normal activity. Normal play was risky for this little boy who had been taught that almost all exploration was wrong. Rodney did improve gradually with new confidence-building efforts, but he remained an inhibited child for at least several years.

Overindulged Children

Karen and Doug Allen had exciting and successful careers. They hoped to raise their children to be happy and successful, too. They wanted their time with them to be joyful and without conflict. Looking back at their own adolescence for parenting guidance, they decided that if their children were given the power to make choices, they would surely be content, and conflict would be minimized.

By ages three and five, Kirt and Liana had developed their choice-making expertise. The problem was that their choice making controlled the household and produced continuous conflict. Here are some choices the children and their parents struggled with:

- Kirt chose not to brush his teeth unless physically forced.
- Liana chose not to eat breakfast unless she had orange soda.

- Kirt chose not to drink his milk unless he was sitting on his dad's shoulders.
- Liana chose not to go to bed unless she was read ten stories.
- Kirt chose not to go to bed unless his mother slept with him.
- Both chose to run around the supermarket unless they were given candy treats.

The list continues. Fortunately the parents received help, and the parents are back in charge. Instead of a three-hour prebedtime battle, the parents now have some evening time to themselves, and the children get a good night's rest. The children feel more secure, and there is much less conflict.

A Sad Story of Too Much Power

Jessica Dubroff's quest for a transcontinental flying record at age seven led to her tragic and untimely death. Her specially fitted Cessna Cardinal permitted her to see over the instrument panel and reach the pedals, and she was accompanied by her flight instructor and her father. However, on the second leg of her journey, her plane crashed in a driving thunderstorm a few minutes after takeoff, killing Jessica and her mentors. "She wasn't forced to fly," said Mark Smith, a pilot who knew the child. He added, "She was seven going on twenty-five."

Jessica was an impressive child who sounded like an adult. Her parents claim they didn't push her. "Jessica set her own goals," those who knew her said, and her parents believed that despite her age, she should have the freedom to make her own choices. Unfortunately, freedom was given beyond Jessica's ability to make responsible decisions.

SOURCE: "Flying Involves 'Tremendously Intense' Choices," by H. E. Nasser and G. Holland, *USA Today*, 12 April, 1996, p. 1A.

The V of Love

The "V of Love" gives you a framework for a global philosophy of discipline. As parents, you've undoubtedly read many books assuring you that you can never love your children too much. Other books have urged you to empower your children. Although you can never love your children too much, be cautious that you empower them carefully and only gradually with the V of Love.

Visualize the letter *V* as a model for guiding the extent of power and freedom given to your children. When your children are very young, they begin at the bottom of the *V*, with limited freedom, power, and few choices. As they grow in maturity and are able to handle more responsibility, the limiting walls of the *V* spread out, giving them gradually increasing freedom and power while still providing parental limits. During adolescence, as your children move to the top of the *V*, they will become capable of considerably more independent decision making and judgment. They will feel trusted by and will continue to respect guidance from their parents and teachers. They will be more competent and have more confidence for moving out of the *V* into adult independence and personal decision making. Thus, freedom and the capability for responsible decision making will increase together and make growing up relatively smooth.

In some families the *V* is reversed to look like this: Λ. Preschoolers who start at the base of this figure are given too much freedom. They have too many choices. They become accustomed to having power and making decisions before they have the wisdom to handle their freedom responsibly. As these children mature, their parents may observe them making poor and even dangerous choices. They worry about the dangers that arise, and argue with them and bribe them. They try to protect them. Thus, these parents curtail their children's freedom and choices, which they hadn't done before. They set limits and take freedoms away. They punish continuously.

As adolescents, they will feel overcontrolled by parents. They'll believe they know more than their parents and teachers. Their angry statements will reflect their feelings of restriction: "My parents are controlling me." "They don't let me do what I want." "They expect me to be perfect." "They used to treat me like an adult and now they treat me like a child." They rebel, feel increasingly angry, or are depressed. They fight their parents and teachers, who should be allowed to guide them. They establish their identity based on what they are opposed to (their parents and teachers) instead of what they are interested in and believe in.

Once freedom is given, it isn't easily taken away. The resulting adversarial mode may force children to rebel, parents to respond negatively, and both to lose the positive home atmosphere that can be so valuable in raising children. Children brought up with the inverted V of Love expend their energies protecting the power they believe they should have. This pattern of protection causes them to engage in power struggles, and often this involves alcohol, drugs, irresponsible sex, and/or violence as sources of temporary power.

The V-shaped love encourages children to develop their talents, freedom, and power responsibly. Developmentally appropriate empowerment is much smoother and more comfortable for children and parents alike, and provides a more comfortable atmosphere in which children can be guided positively. It permits children to enjoy childhood without early adultizement.

Routines and Flexibility

Discipline is made much easier if you use consistent routines most of the time (see chapter 1). Because you also want to teach your preschool children flexibility, you should occasionally vary from these routines so they become accustomed to the concept of making exceptions. For example, you may return from a trip and be very tired, and you usually read to your children before bedtime. You shouldn't feel hesitant to explain that this bedtime will be an exception because "we are all too tired." If they learn the concept of exception, they will be less likely to make a fuss when you make small changes.

Consistency

If you think you're having a problem with being consistent with your preschool children, let me assure you that you're not alone. No parents are entirely consistent. Children don't require absolute consistency, and absolute consistency teaches only rigidity. However, you do have to follow through much of the time if your words are going to be believable to your children. It will help you to be relatively consistent if you do some preplanning. Chapter 7 can help you think through the strategies with which you feel comfortable. After you decide what you think is appropriate for your children, use the same strategies regularly. If you decide to use five minutes of time-out, for example, and you're particularly angry, don't keep adding time or don't threaten to keep your child in her room all night. The threats will only cause your child to be more determined or angry, and you'll probably feel guilty and not follow through and let her out earlier anyway. If you change your consequences once in a while, it won't be disastrous, but if you threaten and change your consequences regularly, your threats will become meaningless. In my clinical work with children, I find that even preschoolers know when they can regularly convince their parents to change decisions.

Summary Advice

- Use your pleasure to encourage appropriate behavior.
- Be disappointed when your children misbehave.
- Make spaces child-safe in order to provide positive discipline.
- Don't provide too much or too little freedom.
- Visualize the letter *V* as a model for how to give freedom and power.
- Use reasonably consistent routines.
- Vary from routines occasionally to teach flexibility.

Mom Can't Discipline Hyperactive Son

Is there any hope for a hyperactive three-year-old boy with a single mom who doesn't understand discipline herself?

You can help your son despite his high energy and your lack of understanding. Start by enrolling in a parenting class in your area specifically for single parents. If you can't find one, check with your local principal. Try to find several other parents who are interested in the class as well. It will provide a fun night out and a support group for your concerns.

Some special tips for you to follow:

Try to be consistent; follow through in setting limits.

Plan each day with alternating play and quiet activities for your son.

Get occasional help with child care so you can take a little time away to be in adult company.

Don't tell your son you feel inadequate; pretend you're in charge even when you feel you're not in control.

Think of some nice things about your son and tell him about
them each day.

As your son gets older, be sure he has some contact with caring
adult males. Teachers, scout and church leaders, and sports
coaches may be helpful.

It is more difficult for a single parent to bring up children, but
many children who have grown up under those circumstances become successful and well adjusted despite the absence of a dad. Be
sure you find a support group, and, of course, believe in yourself
and your son.

Little Girl Chastises Mom

*What should I do when my four-year-old daughter scolds me when
I set limits for her ("Mom, if you talk to me that way, then you
should go to your room and have a time-out")?*

It sounds as if you've already delivered a little too much power
to your daughter, but at age four, that's easy to reverse. During a
quieter time, explain to her briefly that her parents are bigger than
she is because they need to be in charge of guiding her. Someday
when she is older, she will have earned the knowledge to guide her
own children. Remind her briefly that she doesn't have to take a
job or cook meals yet, so she can't tell her parents or other adults
what to do.

Once you've had this discussion with your little girl, don't repeat
it as if it were a lecture. Instead, simply follow through consistently
and ignore her protests. She will soon understand that you are in
charge, and her efforts to control you will dissipate.

It's when a parent assumes that a child should have equal power
that the "adultized" child is in trouble, so be sure not to let her
know that she has you wondering.

5

Appropriate Choices

I t's much in style to give children choices. The belief commonly held by many parents is that if you give children choices they will more likely agree to do what they are supposed to do. Parents also tend to believe that decision making is good intellectual exercise for making intelligent choices later in life. Many parents see giving choices as the best way to teach assertiveness.

The Principle of Choices

Preschool children should be allowed to make some choices. The principle to remember in giving your children choices is to give them only the choices they are capable of making responsibly and not to give them choices when you know what is best for them and the consequences are dangerous or not immediately obvious to the children.

It's inappropriate to believe that natural consequences suffice to teach preschool children how to make appropriate choices. Preschool children are very concrete in their thinking. They cannot project the future yet. The only consequences that affect their further decision making are the consequences that immediately follow their choices, and some of those are too risky and some are too abstract for them to understand.

For example, in childproofing your home (see chapter 6), you put safety plugs into outlets so that children won't get electric shocks during their explorations. The natural consequence, an electric shock, would be immediate and would prevent any further exploration of electrical outlets, but the risks are too great, and children don't have the judgment to make that decision. Your safety plug is used as a limit to prevent an irresponsible choice.

Here's another example: Suppose you decide to give your children choices of anything they want for breakfast, and your daughter picks a chocolate candy bar. The immediate consequence of that choice would be the good sweet taste, and she would undoubtedly choose it again and again if you continued to give her the choices. She cannot automatically know about the poor nutritional value of a chocolate candy bar. If she's accustomed to having all the choices and you said no to her chocolate candy request, the arguments would begin. You can probably hear her now: "It has milk in it, and you give me chocolate milk," or "It tastes better than cereal." And a battle would be on. However, if your daughter is accustomed to your giving her a narrower set of choices— "Would you like cereal or French toast?"—she could make that choice, and you could feel comfortable about giving her either. You have given her a developmentally appropriate choice.

Here's a third, quite common example of giving children appropriate choices: Your four-year-old son takes naps intermittently. He's at the stage where he's almost outgrown napping, but not quite. He seems tired and cranky, and you know a nap would be good for him. If you give him a choice about taking a nap, you can absolutely count on a "no," a power struggle, and tears. Instead, tell him he may choose whether to have quiet time to look at books on his bed or take a nap. He'll remind you that he doesn't want to nap and that he's too big for a nap but will probably be asleep before he finishes his first book. Either choice will be effective. If he doesn't fall asleep during his quiet time, he undoubtedly required only the quiet time, and you can feel confident that he at least had the opportunity to nap.

Preschoolers are capable of making choices between two or three possibilities that are all good for them (as in the cereal–French toast example). By and large, that means you shouldn't ask children if they want to nap, want to go to bed, want to take a bath, want to eat, or want to pick up their toys. These decisions are all your responsibility. As children mature and learn about healthy habits, they'll be in better positions to make these choices responsibly, and you will avoid many of the battles that you see other parents struggle with. In short, don't give choices to children where you will accept only one or you are not being fair. An argument will surely follow.

Parents Need Assertiveness

Sometimes it seems as if in the process of teaching children assertiveness, parents lose their own assertiveness. They are so anxious to please their children, they leave themselves powerless and without family leadership. Children who grow up being given all the choices learn to expect to have all the choices, and that power leaves their parents with very few choices. When you know what's best, be positive and direct, and your children will have confidence in your guidance. They will also feel more secure.

Summary Advice

- Offer children choices appropriate to their developmental responsibility.
- In order for preschoolers to learn from consequences, have consequences follow immediately.
- Offer only choices where all choices they make are appropriate.
- Be positive and direct when you know what's best and children don't.

Girl Insists on Acting Like a Dog

You may laugh when you hear this one. Our daughter, who just turned five, has been acting strange lately. She has always had a love for animals. In fact, what she wanted most for her birthday was a dog. My husband and I both agreed that she wasn't quite ready for the responsibility yet, but promised her that one day we would have one. This is where the strange part comes in.

Ever since this love for dogs came into the picture about six months ago, she's been acting like one, not just pretending for a few minutes, but all day. She goes to the extent of not only crawling on all fours, but lying on the floor with her two arms (paws) in front of her, lying on the very top of the back of the couch, drinking milk out of her glass with her tongue, scratching at the door when she wants to go out, and, to top it off, whining and barking! My husband and I are beside ourselves as to what to do next. We've tried ignoring it, going to the extent of time-outs and not letting her go to friends' houses because of this behavior. HELP! We've always wanted to have a dog, but I sure would like to have a real one and our loving, fun daughter back.

I was a preschool teacher for ten years, so I understand that children need pretend play, but I feel this has gone far beyond that.

Yes, I did laugh at your letter. Lots of jokes came to mind, such as, isn't she "barking up the wrong tree?" or is this a "dog-eat-dog" world? or is her "bark worse than her bite"?

If your daughter is continuing to whine and paw, I expect you're not laughing. So try a private conversation with her something like this:

"We do like your pretend games some of the time, and if you want to, you may play doggie in the morning [or afternoon], but not all day. In the morning, we'll pretend with you, but in the afternoon, we won't, and we won't like it, either. If you keep doing it, we'll certainly think you're too babyish to take care of your own dog, and we won't even think about getting you one while you act this way."

After the conversation, your daughter may wish to talk to you about the issue, or she may even try to negotiate for a dog. Of course, don't negotiate. A "we'll see in the future" is your best response. Continue to permit her to play doggie for a few hours a day, and be sure to ignore or not respond to her barking requests at other times. Ignoring is preferable to punishment, because a power struggle will only prolong the "dog fight." I hope your lovely little girl's return is only a "yelp" away.

A postscript from a six-year-old consultant may also help: She suggested that if you offered your daughter only dog food for her dinner, she would surely stop her barking.

Creative Child Insists on Being Fictional Characters

My four-year-old daughter is gifted, exuberant, funny, strong-willed, and tough-minded. She has assumed the identity of fictional characters since she was two years old, going through Maria (Sound of Music), *Pinocchio, Cinderella, Charlotte, and Dorothy* (Wizard of Oz). *She usually insists on being called by the character of the month and often acts the stories out. Her current identity is Carly, her best friend who is eight. A real person is more complicated. She even insisted on being called Carly when she went back to preschool. She can be very stubborn and demanding about it. Except for occasional tantrums, she is well adjusted. She is an only child, and we are professionals in our forties, happily married.*

Is this going too far? Should we insist on her being called by her real name? I am a psychologist, and this has my colleagues and me baffled!

I always feel a bit awed and flattered when I'm questioned by another psychologist, but I'm pleased to answer your question and hope that you will consider my answer seriously.

Your daughter sounds like a delightful, imaginative child. Creative persons have often had a history of childhood imaginary friends. However, as an only child, there is a great risk of your child becoming "attention addicted" and too powerful. Attention-addicted children frequently feel attention deprived when they enter school, where they must share attention with about twenty-five other children. "Too powerful" children learn to assume that they should do only what they want to do and get angry when they are required to comply with parents, teachers, or friends. If at age four you say your daughter is sometimes "very stubborn and demanding," imagine how those difficult characteristics may worsen by adolescence. You may lose the opportunity to guide her.

Explain to your daughter that you thoroughly enjoy her imaginary play and will be happy to watch her put on her plays for a little time each day. However, also explain that when her pretend play is over, you will again call her by her real name. In preschool, she should expect the same approach. During playtime, she may play pretend, and her playmates may call her Carly or Cinderella or Maria. However, her teachers and friends will call her by her real name when the play is over.

It is important that imaginative children learn to differentiate pretend from real. If they don't, the pretend begins to invade their real lives. They easily extend stories, fabricate, and lie so comfortably and convincingly that it becomes difficult for parents to know when to believe them. Sometimes even the children become confused. While this kind of dishonesty is not intentional and not the same as adult lying, it can easily lead to serious adult problems.

Help your daughter feel secure in her creative play by setting limits for her imagination and by teaching her to identify clearly what is real and what is imaginary. Most of all, enjoy her delightful imagination and encourage her to continue the fun within your safe limits.

Girl Wants to Be Called by Her Middle Name

My four-and-a-half-year-old daughter wants to be called by her middle name, even at preschool. Is this reasonable? She is very serious about this.

You and your daughter's dad named this four-year-old, so don't give her the power to decide her name against your wishes. However, if you like her middle name as well as her first name, she can take her choice with your blessing.

Kids often take on new names and nicknames as they go through school. By the teenage years they may have new preferences, and by adulthood a further selection to match a new, mature identity. Kids can surely call themselves what they wish among their friends. As adults they can, of course, change their names legally. Parents should always have the choice that goes with giving birth and child rearing; that is, calling children by their given name without correction.

At age four, the decisions should definitely be yours. Ignore the protests if you prefer the first name; go along with your daughter if you prefer the middle one.

Nudity Around Preschooler

We have a two-and-a-half-year-old daughter and we have not worried too much about our nudity around her. The question is, what is an appropriate level of nudity around our daughter as she grows?

Alas, I have no correct answer for you, since this is a matter of personal values. Some parents are never concerned about the issue, and others are always concerned. Consider that you are role models for your little girl, but she will not understand limits unless you explain them to her.

If your child attends a preschool, she will certainly need to learn not to touch other children or to permit them to touch her "private parts." The word *private* already suggests a need to cover from view. Surely by kindergarten girls and boys can be taught about privacy. At that point, it continues to be appropriate for adults and children of the same gender to undress together, but for the most part our cultural norms suggest it's time for privacy between the sexes.

Although playing doctor and examining girl/boy differences has gone on forever among small children, in a world that's been hypersensitized to sexual abuse, it is probably healthier for children to learn to cover up by seeing parents who also cover up.

Four-Year-Old Thinks She Still Needs Pacifier

What can I do about my daughter? She is four years old and thinks she still needs a pacifier.

Your Passive Patricia definitely does not require a pacifier, and it should have been taken from her a long time ago. Unless it has inhibited her speech, it has probably not done any great harm despite the fact that it suggests immaturity. If she still uses it during the day, you can wean her off it in a two-step process.

First, insist that the pacifier stays in her room. Permit her to use it in her room for about a month, and then introduce step two. The second step is to explain she is too big to use a pacifier, so you've thrown it away. (Definitely throw it away before you tell her this, so you can be absolute and honest.) Give her a new stuffed animal or doll to replace it as a sleeping partner, and prepare for a few tears or screams. The second night will be easier, and by the third night, you'll wonder why you ever worried.

6

Childproofing: Playpens, Gates, and Fences

P arents can balance freedom and limits during their children's preschool years with childproofing tools such as playpens, cribs, gates, doors, and fences. Children require a place to explore without hearing continuous noes.

The concept of childproofing permits you to remove from reach objects that can cause your children harm while providing a safe area for exploration. It may involve placing such objects out of reach or latching cupboards or covering up areas where exploration could become dangerous. It's always a good idea to leave a drawer or box or cupboard available in each room for distracting children from inappropriate play. Although theoretically young children should be distracted easily, many children display uncanny perseverance when they're determined to explore. If you leave plants within reach, or fragile glass around for children to touch, you will be busy saying no because you've given children choices they're not ready to make.

Restrictions That Allow Freedom

The restrictions of a pen, gate, door, or fence allow children the freedom to check everything in sight, to handle it, to turn it over, or to take it apart. The space within which to explore should be expanded with age. A playpen may work for half an hour or so, but it is restrictive if used for long periods of time or when children are walking or ready to climb out of it. An older child could be allowed to explore a fenced, childproofed play yard with a locked gate. If an eighteen-month-old child is left in a yard where the child can open the gate, all your noes are unlikely to keep that child safe. (See question regarding this situation in the Q&A section at the end of this chapter.) On the facing page is a list that provides suggestions for childproofing.

Adjustable gates can be helpful for keeping children safe and within your sight. The gates that adjust to doorway size and are held in place by spring tension are practical because you can move them from doorway to doorway depending on where you are working or sitting. They require careful installation, because they can be pushed over easily. Furthermore, when using gates you'll need to observe the changes in your children. They may soon become curious and strong enough to push over gates, even if they are properly installed. For these children, only gates that can be fastened onto door frames (and which may mar woodwork) are workable, and for children who may climb over low gates you may have to install a second gate above the lower gate. Circular gates that can provide an outdoor or indoor play yard are also available.

As you can see, gates are variable in their effectiveness. For milder mannered children, they are perfect and will easily provide simple restrictions, while for more aggressive children, only locked doors with safety knobs will prevent their escape from safety.

If you understand the philosophy of freedom and responsibility, you can make better day-to-day decisions of when to allow more freedom, and when to move your children from playpens to gates or doors and to the freedom of the whole house or fenced yard. As

~~~~~~

Tips for Childproofing Your Home

- The goal is to have a home that is safe for preschoolers but still realistically accessible to older children and family members. It is best to sit on the floor and look around each room to see what is at a child's eye level.
- Start with putting the most dangerous items (medicines, cleaning supplies, sharp or breakable items, plants) up high or behind locked cabinet doors. If possible, put them in a separate room that is unavailable to children (locked workshop, parents' bathroom, laundry room, etc.).
- Check for reachable electrical outlets, cabinets, and doors. There are many good kits available to cover standard needs: outlet plugs, cabinet latches, doorknob covers.
- Watch your children play and explore to anticipate potential needs.
- If your are particularly strong and inquisitive, you may need extra measures, such as toilet seat latches, appliance Velcro strips to lock your oven or refrigerator, or magnetized locks.
- Check anything hanging low that could be pulled down on the child or wrapped around the neck: curtain or blind cords, extension cords or wires, and computer accessories, such as printer trays or keyboards.
- Dispose of small round or hard toys or objects that could be choked on. Many toy stores or children's catalogs carry small, inexpensive tubes to use as a size guide with children's game pieces.

Courtesy of Janet Rimm

~~~~~~

you observe your children's intellectual abilities to understand your instructions, you can give them more freedom to explore beyond your walls, as well as trust their judgment to internalize their own self-discipline as they recognize and interpret danger.

There are no exact age guidelines for expanding freedom because your children's temperament and your physical setting will guide you. However, if you give the freedom to your children in small steps, you can pull that freedom back if they don't seem able to cope with it. If you find yourself yelling, screaming, saying no too frequently, or spanking, you know you've given freedom too quickly. Fortunately, during the preschool years, children's resiliency is great, so you can pull in the reins with doors and gates again, and children will soon settle down and feel more secure. You will again be able to be more positive.

Summary Advice

- Use childproofing to allow preschoolers to explore safely.
- Remove harmful and breakable objects.
- Permit more freedom through the use of pens, gates, doors, and fences.
- Increase freedom in small steps as your child's understanding increases.

Toddler Escapes from Play Yard

We live in a housing complex with access to a fenced playground through our back door. Often the gates to the play yard are left open. When my nineteen-month-old daughter finds an open gate, she is out in a flash, running for all she's worth. Once in a while we don't see her leave and then we have to go searching for her, heart in mouth, hoping no one has taken her or that she hasn't headed for the parking lot or that one of the maintenance people in their golf carts or cars haven't run her over. When we find her, we bring her inside the apartment, but I wonder if it is too late to time her out. How do we get a nineteen-month-old to realize she is in danger?

I often ask parents to be less overprotective, but in your case, your daughter needs more protection. A fenced playground would make a good play area for a nineteen-month-old only if you can be 100 percent sure that the gate would not be left ajar or if you could constantly see her through an adjacent window. Your daughter is at real risk because she isn't at an age when she can understand danger. Furthermore, an open gate with you chasing her probably seems like a happy game to her.

In answer to your question, a firm "no" and a brief time-out can be part of your daughter's learning process. Eventually, she will be able to understand the dangers involved in leaving her play yard.

Don't think your daughter is being noncompliant or strong-willed. She is simply exploring and curious and not yet old enough to be responsible for her own safety. To be sure to keep your daughter safe, don't let her explore without your watchful eye on her explorations.

Keeping Toddler Busy in the Kitchen

I have a small kitchen and have placed safety catches on all the cupboards. When I bring toys in for my eighteen-month-old son to play with, he soon loses interest in the toys that are now underfoot. Do you have any ideas for keeping my son busy in the kitchen while I prepare a meal?

Instead of bringing toys into the kitchen, remove the catch from one cupboard that contains pots and pans or plastic ware. If they're all unbreakable, you son will have fun, stay safe, make a mess, but give you enough time to prepare a meal.

7

Rewards and Punishments

Although adults have used rewards and punishments from time immemorial to guide children's learning, new theories and new research show when to use—and when not to use—the commonsense approaches of the past.

Intrinsic Rewards

A target with a bull's-eye provides a model for the continuum and variety of rewards and punishments (see the above illustration). The bull's-eye of the target represents *intrinsic rewards*. Intrinsic rewards are the simple joys of the activity; that is, children develop interests and are engaged. They enjoy what they're doing. The enthusiasm and excitement in learning are intrinsic rewards. Your goal is to encourage many bull's-eye rewards for your children's learning experiences. To see the effects of intrinsic rewards, observe a one-year-old dropping blocks into a container, dumping them, then repeating the activity, or notice a preschooler working industriously to build a sand castle. These children are finding intrinsic rewards. No one is praising them or giving them stickers for their activities.

As in target practice, the bull's-eye is hardest to hit. Furthermore, it isn't possible for all behaviors to be intrinsically rewarding. Some skills that kids may learn are just not fun; for example, picking up toys or making one's bed may not fit into the intrinsically rewarding categories. Tying one's shoe and potty training aren't fun in themselves. There are actually many boring tasks that will never be fun at either home or at school but are nevertheless important for preschoolers to learn.

Attention

The wider circles that surround the bull's-eye of the target are easier and more frequently used by parents, and work better for some tasks. Outside the bull's-eye circle is a circle that represents the second-best tools for rewarding and punishing children; that is, attention given by parents, teachers, and close family members. When important adults are pleased with children's performances, their praise, approval, and interest serve as rewards; their disappointment or lack of interest feel like punishments. Your pleasure and your disappointment are highly effective for motivating your children. Whether or not you use them intentionally to guide them, you should be aware that your children will be sensitive to your feelings and will, for the most part, try to please you if they believe they can. Preschoolers who say, "Do you like my picture?" or "Watch me swim" are asking to be rewarded by attention. It is developmentally natural and healthy for preschoolers to want and need adult attention.

Attention is a powerful reward, and withdrawal of attention is effective for getting children to discontinue behaviors. One-to-one time is the most powerful positive attention you can give children. Positive secrets or plans are effective for getting children to accomplish tasks. Whispering in a child's ears can often get them to give Grandma the kisses they're too busy to give otherwise, and surprising Grandma will add a special note of urgency to giving that kiss. These are forms of very personal, positive parent attention.

Praise. Praise is also a form of positive attention, but praise words have the added effect of setting expectations for your children and teaching them your values. It's for this reason that parents should be wary of competitive or super-praise. Regularly given messages like "You're gorgeous," "the most beautiful child in the world," "the smartest," "the best," or "the best little athlete" can later cause children to believe their parents expect them to be the best. These competitive messages rarely appear to cause harm during the preschool years, but they carry risk into later childhood and adolescence. Children become too competitive or feel inadequate when they believe they cannot meet the high standards they believe their parents have set for them. Children then express anxiety about the pressures they feel, and parents have difficulty understanding why they are being blamed for putting pressure on their children.

High admiration can encourage either motivation or pressure. If children believe they can live up to the high praise, they feel motivated. If they cannot or do not know they can, they feel pressured. In planning for your children, it is good to think about your values and have available some ready praise words that are realistic, positive, and reflect your values so they begin to feel natural to you and effective for setting realistic expectations. Words such as *smart, good thinker, creative, hard worker, kind, sensitive, caring, enthusiastic, helpful, persevering, neat, pretty, strong, brave* are a few of the many positive, nonpressuring words with which you can reward your children.

Referential speaking. A most powerful kind of attention for children is adult talk within their hearing. I've coined the term "referential speaking" to describe conversation between adults when it "refers" to children's behavior or characteristics. Referential speaking is powerful because small children believe that whatever adults say to each other is true; therefore, when adult conversation refers to them, they believe it. If adults tell each other how smart, shy, devilish, restless, or kind children are, the children believe that *is* the way they are. Repeated referential speaking serves as a label to children. Positive referential speaking confers confidence to children, and negative referential speaking is destructive to their self-confidence. They believe they can't change the behavior. When parents, child-care providers, physicians, and relatives use referential speaking carefully, it can make a positive difference in children's healthy growth and development.

Negative attention. Negative attention creates a twofold problem. Because most children crave attention, children who find it difficult to attract positive attention may actually find negative attention rewarding. That doesn't mean they would say they like being scolded, but as a matter of fact research tells us that children tend to continue to behave inappropriately when they are scolded overtly in a group. Indeed, their behavior worsens the more they are scolded. Quiet signals or secrets are much more effective in getting them to stop their inappropriate behaviors.

The other disadvantage of continuous negative put-downs and reprimands is that these children feel as if they are expected to behave badly. In your own home or in a preschool environment, they develop the feeling of being known as the "bad kid." Thus, continually calling your children "slobs," "mean," "troublemakers," "little devils," "klutzes," "lazy," or "stupid" may cause problems for children for the rest of their lives. I remember so clearly a difficult fourteen-year-old who came to my clinic recalling how his problems began in first grade, how he got the reputation for being a troublemaker, and how that reputation seemed to follow him no matter how he tried to escape it. Most children can't tell you about how that happens to them, but it surely does, and it can be prevented with some conscientious effort. What you say to children directly and what you say to other adults in that children's presence sets important positive or negative expectations for them. It is powerful attention.

Consequences

The third circle of the target, representing the natural consequences of an activity, provides the next most effective category of rewards and punishments. Children who dress themselves independently come to preschool feeling better than the children who are nagged each morning. The former are experiencing positive consequences; the latter, negative consequences. Children who start fights suffer the consequences of starting those fights. Other children will fight back or say mean things to them. Children who share with the other children are more likely to make friends.

Consequences are the automatic reward or punishment if they immediately follow preschool children's activities. Abstract or future consequences are not meaningful to preschool children. If parents and teachers want to make future consequences more meaningful to preschoolers, they will have to explain the relationship between the activity and the consequence quite concretely; for example, "Joshua hit you today because you were mean to him yesterday."

Activities

The personal attention of important adults and immediate consequences are preferable to the two outer reward and punishment rings of the target. The fourth ring represents activities as a reward for children's learning performance and withdrawal of activities as a punishment. The daily schedule in chapter 1 and the bedtime routines in chapter 18 use activities as natural rewards; for example, "When you finish your snack, we'll read a book." Preschools also use activity rewards effectively: "After we clean up the toys, we'll have our snack."

Parents tend to use—or overuse—the withdrawal or punishment component of activities more frequently than the reward component. Parents frequently take away activities for long periods of time. Although removal of activities is much more effective than spanking or screaming, parents should be careful to remove these activities briefly—taking television away for for one show or for one day will make your point. Taking television away for a full week also makes your point clear, but it provides no motivation for your child's improved behavior the next day. Furthermore, if parents keep adding a day for bad behavior, kids give up in despair and think there's no longer a reason to try to do better, or they dig in their heels and accelerate the battle.

Material Rewards

The final and largest ring of the target is related to the use of material rewards and punishments, which may include stickers, baseball cards, stars, points, money, gifts, etc. Technically, these are referred to as "token reinforcements" and are probably used most frequently by all parents. Token reinforcements are effective for short-term purposes. However, they can be overused. Children may learn to negotiate tokens or become dependent on their use.

Token rewards are most effective when they're used temporarily as a bridge to the inner circles of the target and when other, less tangible rewards don't work.

Overuse. Overusing material rewards may result in unintentionally teaching children to manipulate adults for gifts. Sometimes children who have received gifts for learning letters, for example, will ask for bigger gifts the next time they learn something, or they may refuse to learn unless they are promised gifts. Sometimes children refuse to eat or sleep unless given a prize. You can see that using gifts too much may backfire. Many parents use the two outer circles of the target most often. As you gain expertise in parenting, you'll find yourself using the three inner circles more frequently.

The organizing of a preschooler's day described in chapter 1 incorporates natural and simple consequences and attention to daily routines. The use of regular expectations can eliminate many of the token rewards or punishments. During the preschool years, stickers, smiley faces, and stars are nice, simple rewards if you feel like your children need encouragement for toilet training, sleeping through the night, or picking up their toys. Your approval and moderate praise, however, are usually quite sufficient.

Summary Advice

- Children's natural interests are the best rewards.
- Moderate praise and positive attention are effective rewards.
- Overpraise may cause pressure.
- Negative attention encourages negative behaviors and expectations.
- Natural consequences can be effective only if they are immediate.
- Explain the relationship of behavior to consequences.
- Design daily routines that are rewarded by natural activities.
- Don't overuse activities as punishments.
- Don't overuse large material rewards.
- Preschool children enjoy simple token rewards like stickers, stars, and smiley faces.

Girl Who Won't Talk

I am a seasoned teacher, as well as director of a nursery school. I teach four-year-olds. This year I have a little girl who will not open her mouth. Her mother (also a teacher) and I are very frustrated. I honestly feel she is being stubborn and acting this way for attention. I have run the gambit from every positive persuasive idea and antic to, I must admit, anger. The child is mature and intelligent enough to recognize that my anger was well based; she accepted it without a word or flinching, and there were no tears (she did not feel that I was unfair). I feel I spend too much time with her some days, trying to draw her out and adding to her special attention. I must add that in a controlled classroom with seventeen other four-year-olds who care about her and try to help me help her, we would all stand on our heads if we knew it would help.

This same child is very verbal at home. She is extremely shy when she attends social gatherings with her family but does talk with familiar people. I am most distressed, and I would appreciate any insight into helping my little friend that you can offer.

The term "elective mute" is given to children who choose not to talk in particular environments, although they are quite capable of speech in other environments. I have had good success in working with such children by first asking all adults not to talk about the lack of speech within their earshot. Referential discussion at home among adults, as well as talk between teachers and students, should be eliminated. If other students ask you why this student isn't talking, respond briefly by explaining that she'll talk when she wishes to and that there's no reason to worry or talk about it.

In a private conference with the little girl, explain that she may choose to talk whenever she's ready, and it's entirely up to her. Add that you will put a star on a card whenever she speaks up in class, but that you won't tell anyone about the card until she gets five stars. When she has earned five stars, you'll let her parents know, because they may wish to give her a small reward.

Now all you need to do is relax, and you will see it happen. After a few weeks, she'll speak up. Don't bring any attention to it except to secretly show her the star card. She'll continue to talk after the first five stars, and soon you may wonder how you can manage to get her to stop talking.

The behavior modification star card is not the real key. It is the elimination of all the referential talk. Too much talk about not enough talk causes kids to feel they can't do anything about their problem. Also, your asking other students to help her with the problem as well as the likely attention to the problem have unfortunately prolonged it.

Oversensitive Preschooler

Our four-and-a-half-year-old daughter seems to be overly sensitive. Whenever she's playing with other children in a group, she gets jealous and cries easily. What can we do to handle this situation?

Some children adjust more easily to sharing and socializing than others, but you will surely want to help your daughter learn to share attention before she enters kindergarten. Begin by inviting only one of her friends to your home to play with her. Before her friend comes, explain to your daughter briefly and privately how important it is to take turns in play and how she should even occasionally offer her turns to her friend. Here's an example of how she could give her friends choices: "Would you like to play with my dolls, or would you like to play outside on the swings?"

Let your daughter know that if you notice her sharing, you'll give her a private signal (a pat on her shoulder) once in a while, but if she's crying or upset, you'll quietly escort her to her room for a little time alone to calm herself. You can tell her she can come out and join her friend again as soon as she feels better. Be very specific and concrete with your instructions.

By using private signals, you'll be helping her to improve her social skills without giving her negative attention. After she improves her relationship with one child, invite two (not one) more children. Even-numbered groups work better than odd ones.

Any discussions with her about the problem should be brief, and be sure to emphasize her positive improvements. When you talk to other adults within her hearing (referential speaking), don't talk about her social problem. Instead, casually comment on how much better she's doing. You're likely to see rapid improvement.

Climber

My four-year-old daughter climbs on everything: cupboards, vanity, tables, chairs, everything that is dangerous. I've tried many different solutions and nothing works. Do you have any answers?

High-energy children are a challenge to parents and need a tremendous amount of consistency. Timing her out in her room every time she climbs will undoubtedly be much more effective than continuous scolding.

Also, eliminate adult talk within her hearing about her out-of-control climbing, and I emphatically stress that you don't refer to her as a "little monkey" or any other such term. Discussion about her continuous climbing sets expectations for her and gives her recognition for her out-of-control activity. "Little monkey" can serve as a label for a climber, and she'll surely enjoy living up to her label.

Be sure to take her to the playground and allow her to climb safely on playground equipment. Preschool gymnastics, swimming, and dance are also appropriate fun outlets for the exercise of her coordination skills.

8

To Spank or Use Time-Out

E ven in these politically correct times, there is hardly a parent
who hasn't ever spanked a child. There are times when at least
one of your children was exasperating and you were at the edge
of your temper and slapped a hand or spanked a bottom. It isn't
likely that a few spankings or slaps on the hand destroyed your
children or your relationship with them. Yet, it's even less likely
that spankings or slaps improved your ability to discipline your
children or improved your family relationships. If you've slipped
and spanked a few times, forgive yourself, but have a different plan
for the future. There are many alternatives.

A No-Win Situation

The slap or spanking may do more to benefit or punish the person
doing the spanking than it does for the child. It's pretty much a no-
win situation. If a parent believes spanking is the right thing to do,

he or she will probably increase the spankings, and the angry relationship between parent and child will fester and decrease the possibility of the parent becoming a good role model.

Research tells us that it's likely children will learn that hitting is an acceptable way to deal with controversy if they are hit. They will become more aggressive and take out the anger on other children or adults. If the parent feels guilty about the spanking, he or she will undoubtedly apologize to the child, and during the preschool years when children think so concretely, they'll feel confused about why the parent is apologizing to them for something they did wrong. No good results seem to come from using corporal punishment with children.

"Spare the rod and spoil the child" may have fit well in another era, when, after a child was spanked, a parent's threat would be enough to deter a child from further naughty behavior. Sometimes a parent would raise a wooden spoon in the air or take off a belt as if ready to spank. The child would typically become immediately compliant out of fear. Threats were so effective that very few actual spankings needed to take place.

In the present world of overempowered children and continued exposure to media violence, however, the first spanking rarely stops the behavior. It is almost as if the child is determined not to show the pain and defy the parent. Sometimes children laugh when they're spanked, but the laughter only displays the tension and confusion they feel. The child's laughter upsets parents even further and they spank harder. Sometimes little kids even try to hit back, and although their little hands don't invoke much pain, their hitting further aggravates parents. It is similar to two children fighting, except the difference in size is painfully obvious and absurd.

Even if children's behaviors are deterred by spankings and their behavior improves, you can expect to see spanked children act out the effect of the spanking by spanking their dolls, pets, siblings, and even friends. Spanking seems to be contagious. It is much better and safer to use other limits.

Parental Disagreement

Spanking causes the most problems in families where the parents disagree about its use. If Dad insists on spanking, Mom will either sit by feeling frustrated or protect the child by explaining that

"Daddy didn't mean it" or "It wasn't right for Daddy to spank you." This causes an alliance between Mom and the child against Dad and gives the child more power than Dad. Mom is also giving a message of disrespect for Dad, thus nullifying the preventative effect of the spanking. That can cause Dad to spank more and harder because he believes the child has ignored him and is being deliberately disobedient and requires further punishment. The child often cries even harder to get Mother's attention and protection.

The best approach for Mom is to support Dad during that initial spanking. If the child comes to Mom to complain about Dad's spanking, it would be better to say something like, "If you listen to Dad the first time, he won't ever have to spank you again." That support is less likely to cause a second spanking. Then, of course, Mom and Dad should talk over their differences. If they can't resolve those differences, they should go to a counselor for help in becoming united in their approach to discipline.

The Risks of Abuse

Real life may be much more complicated than my case example. Dad may spank despite Mom's support or objection. He may refuse to go to a counselor and insist on continuing the spankings. Although spanking is not in itself abuse, preschool children are so small and helpless, and the spanker sometimes becomes so angry, that the spanking could accelerate, could develop into shaking, hitting hard, kicking, and could become physical abuse. If the spanker is under the influence of alcohol or drugs, the risk increases. Physical abuse is very serious. Mother will need to make some difficult and rapid decisions. If this is happening in your home, you must take the courage to protect your child. If your child is being abused, it is best to go into a room with the child and lock the door. Call 911 as quickly as you can get to a telephone.

If you're not certain whether your child is being abused, the best place to start is with a counselor. The counselor can help you determine the next step. If, in fact, your child is being abused and you fear reprisal, then you must seek shelter for yourself and your child. There are shelters in all large and even medium-size cities for families who require immediate protection, and the staff can help you plan for a safer future.

Providing Safety and Adult Care

During such stressful times in life, mothers often find themselves confiding in their children, particularly the oldest children in the family. There is a great risk in this confidence. It will be difficult to convince the child ever to trust or respect the abusive parent, even if the parent gets help and changes. Furthermore, once a child is empowered as an adult, the mother will seem powerless to the child. It will be difficult for the child to trust the mother, either. The child is likely to become disrespectful to both parents. Children do, of course, require help and explanation at this time. It is better that preschool children are not given intimate details, which they may be unable to cope with or understand. It is most important that the mother gain her strength and support through other adults: friends, parents, or counselors can be helpful. Abuse is frightening and lonely, and adults need support and safety. Children require safety and the security of knowing that a loving, strong adult will continue to care for them.

Time-Out

A better alternative to spanking is using time-out. Time-out can be effective for preschool children if it is used appropriately and not used too frequently. Overuse of time-out occurs because of poor planning and is counterproductive, causing parents to believe time-out isn't effective. Also, many inappropriate behaviors by a child may be ignored or walked away from. In effect, you may wish to time yourself out in order to let your child work through frustration or conflict.

Cribs, chairs, and bedrooms. A toddler's crib works extremely well as a first time-out location. Logically one would think that the crib might then be connected with punishment and would prevent the warm, positive association you would like to provide for the child's naps and bedtime. Strangely enough, that doesn't seem to happen. Although I've recommended a crib time-out to thousands of families, I have never heard of a single crib phobia. Of course, if a child does develop fear of a crib, you should not use it for time-out. When cribs are used to time out children for biting or hitting, toddlers seem to cry or fall asleep, but it doesn't seem to interfere with their normal comfort within the crib. Furthermore, after a few brief uses, children seem to associate time-out with the idea that they are not supposed to bite or hit. A crib is a safe place for children's time-out and clearly limits the child's continued negative behavior.

When children outgrow their cribs, a time-out chair seems to be the next useful tool. A small chair can be placed in a room away from the central activities of the home. Some parents have used the steps leading upstairs, which seems to be effective if the child is out of the family mainstream.

Using a timer. A timer works well for time-out. When children hear the buzzer, they know they may leave their time-out chair. Preschool children require only a short time for time-out, and it is important to avoid leaving a child in time-out for long periods of time. Five minutes or less for a preschooler seems adequate to make the point that they must discontinue the inappropriate behavior.

Understanding the reason. It is important that children understand the reason they are being timed out. The first time a child commits a particular misbehavior, an explanation should be given and a substitute behavior should be taught to the child. For example, if a child grabs another child's toy, he should be instructed to share, and the concept of taking turns should be simply explained. If the child then repeats the grabbing behavior, time-out should be used. A parent could simply say, "You must take turns" or "You may not grab Charlie's truck" while timing out. There would be no need for a lengthy explanation the second time; one or two sentences would be enough. No further statement after the buzz of the timer is necessary. If the child has hit or hurt someone and is verbal, it would be appropriate for the child to apologize at this time.

Overempowered children. When children don't stay in their chairs or sit on the steps, the next place for time-out is in a separate room. Often the child's own bedroom works well. There isn't any reason to clear out toys. The purpose of time-out is to limit inappropriate behavior, rather than actually punish. Even if toys are in their room, they get the idea that the behavior must stop.

Most children will stay in their rooms without gates or doors when told they must go to their room, and they will think about how they can do better next time. If not, a gate that separates the child from a parent's attention seems to stop a problem after a time or two. For children who climb over gates, a double gate vertically installed is usually effective. While it's true children probably don't spend a lot of time thinking about the problem, it is usually clear that their behavior is not approved of and must stop. If they're angry, children should be given permission to cry, lose their temper privately in their rooms, or punch a pillow. It's not a good idea to talk things over with children when they're angry or to comfort and hold them because they didn't get what they wanted. Discussion only ends in an irrational power struggle and comforting serves to reinforce or encourage further negative behavior. It is better to save talk for later when children are calm.

If children are so overempowered that they will not stay in their rooms, a specially designed time-out is appropriate. The locked-door time-out (described in my book *Dr. Sylvia Rimm's Smart Parenting*) is to be used specifically to rein in the power of the children who are out of control. A locked-door time-out is extremely helpful for regaining control of overempowered children, but it is unnecessary for more compliant children.

Whichever form of time-out you plan to use, if you've explained to your children beforehand, when they are calm, what will happen during time-out, they are more likely to accept time-out as a way to handle their anger and discontinue the naughty behavior. Some specific examples of time-out use are given in later chapters.

Summary Advice

- Don't spank or slap your children.
- Parents should resolve their differences about spanking.
- Spanking can lead to abuse.
- Seek shelter from an abusive parent.
- Find support through other adults rather than children.
- Time-out is more effective than spanking.
- Use a crib for timing out toddlers.
- A chair or a child's room is effective for time-out.
- Permit children to express their anger in their rooms.
- Save talk for when children are calm.
- Explain to your children beforehand how time-out works.

Dominating Mother

I am very concerned about my granddaughter. She is three years old and since birth her mother has been an overpossessive, dominating parent. When her father would try to discipline her, her mother would tell him to shut up or leave her alone. Her mother sleeps with her, lets her stay up until eleven at night and sleep until ten in the morning. My granddaughter will not give her father a kiss or show any affection toward him. This hurts his feelings very much.

She is at home with her mother during the day, and her mother is constantly spanking and hollering at her. She acts silly and talks like a little baby. I would like your advice.

Your are in a helpless position in terms of giving parenting advice. I assume your granddaughter's mother is your daughter-in-law and not your daughter; therefore, you need to have a private talk with your son. Explain to him that you don't wish to cause any problems, but you believe he and his wife need help with their parenting skills, and you are not in a position to give it. Suggest they seek outside counseling. Your granddaughter's baby talk and your daughter-in-law's need to spank for control can be explained as reasons for them to go for parenting therapy. If your son can't convince his wife that they need counseling, an excellent alternative for them is to attend parenting classes.

If indeed your observations are accurate, your grandchild may be in trouble. If the spanking gets out of control, and you're worried about the safety of your granddaughter, as difficult as it may be, you should call Social Services to report the suspected abuse.

Boy Who Won't Sleep

Our son is three years old. He refuses naps and gives me a hard time at bedtime every night. We have always had difficulty getting him to sleep, but until just recently, he couldn't open his bedroom door. Now that he can, he just won't stay in his room. No amount of bribing, pleading, talking, or discipline seems to help. I have spanked him for not staying in his room. When he comes out, I take him back and warn him that if he comes out again, he will get a spanking. He comes out anyway! I feel very bad about spanking him, and I don't want to do it, but I don't know any alternatives. He refuses a nap, so I usually put up a gate in front of his door so he has to at least stay in his room for a while. Today, he broke the gate and came sneaking into the living room.

My husband and I are at wit's end over the right kind of discipline to use. Our son is very loving and otherwise listens well. I hope you will reply so my husband can see an answer.

Many children push bedtime limits. They seem energetic, tireless, and anxious to be little adults, even at age three. They often want to stay with their parents until their parents go to sleep. While all this seems natural, parents who yield to their children's pressure find themselves feeling overwhelmed and cheated.

Once bedtime rituals are firmly established, they can become pleasant ends to the day. Be sure to make exceptions to the routines for special occasions, but if there are no routines, there can be no exceptions. If children regularly control their own bedtimes, evenings soon become full of struggles, and morning wake-ups feel impossible. The children soon describe themselves as "night people," and the parents describe themselves as "always tired people."

Explain to your son that he must go to sleep on time because he needs his sleep, and you and his dad need quiet time together. Expect to see a few tears; he'll probably cry or complain. Suggest that he hug some stuffed animals, and indicate you'll be happy to leave a light on in his room if he'd like. Explain to him that you'll leave his door open if he can fall asleep quietly, but will close and lock it if he cries, screams, or tries to come out of his room. Assure him that you'll open the door when he's quiet. Then give him a good-night hug and a smile that masks the mixture of anxiety and anger you feel, and leave the room.

If he gets out of bed and follows you, take him back to bed and close the door. Leave a light on so he isn't frightened. Fisher-Price makes a plastic safety knob that fits over the doorknob and prevents a child from being able to open the door. If that doesn't work, tie a piece of rope around his outside doorknob, and attach it to another doorknob. Don't stand at the door holding it closed. That would only become a power struggle you'd lose. Be prepared. Your son will likely cry and scream the first time. Don't respond. You've prepared him well. He will finally fall asleep, although you may find him on the floor near the door.

When all is quiet, be sure to open the door. As you arrange the covers around your sleeping angel, you'll have the satisfaction of knowing you've taught him to take an important, difficult step toward independence. By the second night, he'll go to sleep with no more than a whimper, and although he may complain for a few days about the difficulty of falling asleep, he'll soon learn he cannot manipulate bedtime, and you may again enjoy your much-deserved adult time together at the end of a hard workday.

The regimen that you and your husband have already tried includes far too much talk, unnecessary arguing and spanking, and far too many battles that your three-year-old has won. Be firm and calm and win this one with confidence. Your son will gain a new respect for limits, and you'll find you can again enjoy him because you're in charge and he's more rested.

Aggressiveness Toward Sister

I have a three-year-old son and an eight-month-old daughter. My son has always been very active. He enjoys lots of activity, people, and attention. On the other hand, my daughter is quiet, easygoing, and enjoys playing independently.

The problem is my son will not leave our daughter alone and is physically aggressive. He still asks when we're going to take her back to the hospital. He demands to be the center of attention even among our friends and family. My husband is frequently away from home days at a time. My son's behavior seems worse when my husband is gone.

We use a combination of time-out techniques and spanking (as a last resort) for disciplinary measures, but some days it seems like an endless battle! Any suggestions?

Time-outs will work if you use them consistently for your son's aggressive behavior. Spankings aren't effective and will only model more aggressive behavior. The more you spank, the more he'll hit.

Your son needs some help in learning positive alternatives for playing with his little sister. Patting and kissing her will help him express affection he'll soon learn to feel. You may even wish to let him hold his sister on his lap for a few minutes so you can compliment him on his being a "big helper." Some special one-to-one time with you while the baby is asleep will also feel reassuring to your son. Insist on quiet time alone for everyone for a little part of each day. Gates across the doorways of each of your children's rooms can accommodate their quiet times. Toys for your son to play with while he is in his room can make his time alone pleasant. He'll cry the first time, but you can explain before you close the gate that mommies need time alone, too. If you don't respond to his tears, he'll settle down and play. After two or three times, he'll get the idea and play without crying. It's a good idea for you to wean him from constant attention now because attention-dependent children do not adjust well to sharing attention when they begin school.

When you talk to other adults about your children (referentially), be sure to emphasize the positive relationship between your son and his sister and avoid mentioning the sibling rivalry. If your son hears you talking about his aggressive behavior, he'll be more likely to live up to that negative image. Right now your son may feel like he's a "bad boy" compared to his sister. If you can stay patient and positive, he'll soon accept his sister, although like most older brothers, he'll probably do his share of teasing, fighting, and, fortunately, also loving.

Time-Out Away from Home

You have addressed the issue of time-out for misbehavior in your column before. However, what means does a parent use to discipline a strong-willed son who misbehaves away from home? What is to be done when he behaves badly in the supermarket or at the homes of friends or relatives?

Strong-willed children seem to have a special sensitivity to their parents' vulnerability. It's as if they realize that your limit setting is less powerful when you're in public. You will want to prepare ahead so that you're not caught unprepared. When there is no time-out room available, small rewards work best.

Before you begin shopping, explain to your son that you know he really wants to behave, and give him specific guidelines for what you expect; for example, stay seated in the cart or stay in the same aisle as you, don't touch items on the shelves unless you ask for his help, and so on. As you explain how much you appreciate his shopping company, offer him the opportunity to pick out a small special treat when you're finished shopping, provided he's behaved well. You'll need to be consistent in following through. If he hasn't earned his treat, his tantrum will only come at the end of your shopping trip. Then you'll be able to escort him to a time-out at home immediately afterward. However, don't be surprised if your treat, in combination with your positive planning, is effective—it almost always works.

If you're visiting friends or relatives, you may also use the treat approach. However, if these are close friends with children of their own, you may ask to borrow their time-out room if necessary. You are clearly not the only parents with a strong-willed child, but you'll have to assess the appropriateness of your request in each family situation.

Timing out when a child gets home is never quite as powerful. A warning to your son that a negative consequence will await him will be even more effective than telling him exactly what you intend to do. When he challenges you by asking what you're planning, keep him wondering by explaining that you're giving it some thought. Your pondering and his wondering are far more effective than threats of overpunishment, which he realizes you may not carry out.

A strong-willed child sometimes feels more like a challenge than a joy, but beneath his powerful facade is your wonderful son. If you can manage to stay both positive and firm, you'll reach the "sweet kid" within more frequently.

Angry, Negative Boy

How can I prevent my three-year-old son from projecting his anger in a negative way? He has seen this behavior modeled by the other men in the family. I'd like him to be more in control emotionally when he gets upset. Also, how can I teach my daughter to handle the angry verbal abuse from my son (or any other males) in the future?

I perceive that you are indeed tired of receiving and observing anger in men and also want to protect your daughter from similar experiences. Although none of us should have to be continual recipients of anger from our partners, parents, and friends, occasional losses of temper are certainly human, and we do need to learn to avoid internalizing those as our problems.

For your son, you can teach him early to handle his temper privately by timing him out in his room. Discussion of the topic may happen later if he is calm. It would be important for him not to get his way when he loses his temper. His sister can learn to protect herself by going into her room or yours for privacy and protection if her brother is verbally abusive toward her. That will frustrate him, of course, but he will soon stop.

As for the adult men in the family, the options are much different. If anger is addressed to you, you need to have an open conversation with the adult at a time when he is calm. Come to some agreement about what he and you will do when he loses his temper. Explain that you can't possibly communicate under those circumstances and definitely don't internalize this as your own problem. You may need a counselor's help in developing more reasonable communication skills.

As for your daughter, she'll need to be sure to be respectful when Dad scolds her, to do what he asks unless she thinks it's unreasonable. However, don't let her decide that anything she doesn't feel like doing is unreasonable. Don't be overprotective about her dad, or she will use his losses of temper to get you to side with her against him. On the other hand, if he is truly abusive, she needs protection, and she should be able to come to you for that. You will need to assess carefully if she's manipulating or whether she does need your safety net. You will also want to let her know that she shouldn't tolerate verbal abuse from others, and you'll be there to help her if she really is in trouble.

There is a fine but important line between verbal abuse and the very human loss of temper that every parent experiences. You become the important interpreter to your children of which adult anger is extremely unfair and which overreactions are reasonable responses to frustration.

Mini-Time-Out for Toddler

My son is fifteen months old and he's starting to misbehave. I think he's too young for time-outs. I'm wondering if there is a mini-time-out for when he's two, and if I use his crib, would there be any risk of his being afraid of his crib?

Even at fifteen months, toddlers require limits. However, they're a little young to time-out. Usually distraction (another toy) and childproofing his environment take care of most of the limit setting. Distraction is amazingly effective since little guys his age concentrate on one thing at a time, and involvement with a new toy seems to prevent any further naughty activity.

As he gets a little older, a mini-time-out may be in order after several unsuccessful distractions or naughty behaviors. Of course, you're right that his crib is an ideal location. Leave a few toys for him to play with. He may cry a little or just play. Sometimes toddlers fall asleep because the "naughtiness" was actually sleepiness. No special timing is required; nor is a closed door. Because your little fellow will either be happily playing for a while or napping, it results in absolutely no crib trauma, although it does set a reasonable limit.

When your little boy moves to a bed in which he might not stay if timed out, be sure his room is child-safe and put a gate at the door. Stay out of view. Closing the door might be frightening to a two-year-old, and the gate will be sufficient to set an appropriate limit. A two-year-old needs only a few minutes of settling down before he can come out. Time-outs are so much more humane than the confusing anger, warnings, overreasoning, and more anger that are often typical.

9

Team Support

It is unlikely that there has ever been in any culture the complexity of child care that takes place for many families in our society today. It would be difficult to list the variety of child-care arrangements that affect preschool children in these complex times. Chapter 10 will deal with selecting child care and chapter 11 will emphasize communicating with child-care providers. This chapter will emphasize the importance of working as a team for your children's benefit.

No sports team ever won a game when team members expended their energies attacking or undercutting one another. No family or children make gains or are happier when those responsible for their love and care expend their energies sabotaging each other's power or competing with each other to be the better caregiver. Raising mentally healthy children is a team effort.

Team Involvement by Fathers

The role of fathers in the family has changed dramatically from only a generation ago and even more dramatically compared to that of your grandparents. The change usually delights mothers and fathers alike.

Although fathers have not yet established that they can become pregnant, they share readily in the announcement of pregnancy. The announcement is more typically "We're pregnant," rather than "My wife is pregnant," and fathers often share in preparatory classes during pregnancy and are likely to be nearby helping and encouraging during delivery. The result seems to provide a memorable bonding experience for all and much more of a team.

The good news is that many dads do almost everything. The exception, of course, is breast-feeding. If they've observed their friends involved in fathering, they are likely to participate automatically and without prompting. If he is a first dad in the neighborhood and his dad wasn't involved, parenting skills may not seem natural to him and he may be more anxious about taking full responsibility. Encouraging participation early is most effective even if Dad fears that the baby will break at his touch. After all, new mothers often feel that way as well. It will probably help new dads to know that mothers are anxious, too.

If you're a mom who's married to a dad who resists fatherhood out of fear or discomfort, a good conversation may set him at ease. You may also want to share your knowledge a small step at a time to help him build confidence. Be sure to leave Dad alone with your preschooler some of the time. Bonding doesn't take place with continual Mom intervention. The everyday care involved in serving meals and helping with dressing helps fathers feel natural about their parenting. Joint shopping trips, work projects, games, and stories cement relationships. Paired experiences with cooking and laundry help your children to grow up without the gender stereotypes that their dads grew up with. Dads taking kids to work occasionally (if their jobs permit) also allows children to see their dads in a different environment. Relationships with fathers are important for both girls and boys, as are relationships with mothers.

Fatherhood has done much to broaden the potential expression and self-fulfillment of both men and women. Although involvement needs to continue and increase, it is probably one of the many and marvelous contributions of the feminist movement.

Communication

Teaming takes a game plan and involves good communication. Neither parents, grandparents, nor child-care providers are equipped for mind reading. Furthermore, there is more than one right way to bring up children, and it's not unusual for adults to disagree on the day-to-day care of children—and they may all be right. Many alternatives exist. As discussed earlier, although no parent is absolutely consistent, reasonable consistency is important for children at least to the point where adults don't give directly opposite messages to them. If the adults consistently contradict one another, children learn to manipulate the people in their environment to get what they want. Children's wants are typically for immediate gratification, because they are not yet able to predict the future. The person who gives them what they want in direct opposition to what another adult told them they couldn't have effectively sabotages the other adult's power. The person who gives in feels like a good parent, but the other adult will feel powerless, or like a fifth wheel. Children actually become "adultized"—more powerful than a parent or caregiver. Here's a common example:

> Bill James is a dentist. He's very concerned about the effects of sweets on children's teeth. He and Marge Todd-James have agreed not to give their preschoolers sweets except on the weekend. Grandma Todd, who knows of the parents' policy, brings a box of candy as a gift for the family and insists it won't hurt the children to have a little extra candy that week. Marge is in the middle. Grandma effectively sabotages Dad, and the children think Grandma is great and consume candy all day with her permission and a wink of the eye. Eating the candy is, of course, not a life-threatening misdemeanor, but the team cocaptains have been sabotaged. A brouhaha of disrespect will undoubtedly follow by evening, and the dad will be diminished in his children's eyes. While Grandma was feeling good about her special Grandma privilege, her son-in-law was wishing

she'd not visit, and Marge was wondering why her husband was so fussy about the sweets and why her mother couldn't bring another gift to the children. This team will falter; the children simply won't know which captain to follow.

How It Feels

You can certainly relate to this story better if you're the team captain who is being undercut. You may indeed feel angry about what is happening to you on a daily basis at the hands of your husband, mother, mother-in-law, or nanny. But if you're the adult doing the undercutting, you're probably thinking, "What's the big deal? It's only a little candy (or money or special permission)." You probably believe you're in the right because you decide the other person is "too rigid," "too controlling," or "too strict." It feels comfortable because you feel like the good adult. If that is the case, return to the sports team analogy: team sabotage just doesn't work, and family sabotage doesn't, either. It fosters manipulative and rebellious children who grow up with little respect for the adults who must guide them. Although an occasional slip will undoubtedly cause no major problems, consistent family sabotage creates dysfunctional families for generations. (More detailed information is available on these sabotage rituals—called "ogre and dummy games"—in my *Why Bright Kids Get Poor Grades and What You Can Do About It* and *Dr. Sylvia Rimm's Smart Parenting*.) Consistent family sabotage fosters highly rebellious children.

Respect

If you would like your children to respect the adults who teach and lead them, the adults must show respect for one another. If parents are disrespectful to each other by permitting children to ignore each other's guidelines, children are learning disrespect and will voice disrespect for the whole team. You might try the experiment of describing your spouse or parent in positive ways within your children's hearing. You will soon see your children gaining in respect for the entire parenting team. Being respectful is contagious.

Summary Advice

- Support the team effort in raising your children.
- Communicate sensitively and carefully.
- There are many right ways to bring up children.
- Don't undercut a parent or grandparent.
- Family sabotage causes child rebellion.
- Teach respect by being respectful.

Boy Prefers Dad

My husband and three-year-old son have a very close relationship, for which I am thankful. When we are all together, however, my son consistently will ask me to leave and if he is hurt or sad, prefers my husband. I try to be matter-of-fact about this, but I feel left out at times. I'm going back to work full time soon. I don't want to feel even more left out. Any advice?

Many small children today have close relationships with their dads that are different than what was typical a generation ago, when mothers were the primary caregivers for preschool children. Back then, it was always more usual for children to run to their mothers for sympathy, and I expect the dads sometimes felt like fifth wheels. Even though it hurts a little, try to feel pleased that your husband and son have such a good relationship. As long as your husband is respectful and loving toward you, your son will soon learn to be less exclusive in his relationship with his dad.

To cultivate your own close relationship with your son, reserve some special times when you and he can become involved in activities together. Playing board games, involving him in imaginative play, or walking together to enjoy the outdoors go a long way in establishing a bond with either parent.

Returning to full-time work will help you build personal confidence and will not harm your relationship with your son as long as you allow some time after work for special activities, which will keep you close. Ask whomever is caring for him during the day to keep a daily record of the cute things he says, the new skills he learns, and his daily activities while you're at work. If you can read them each day, it will help you to stay in touch with his development and interests and will assist you in feeling like the important balancing wheel that you truly are.

Incessant Whining

Our four-year-old whines continuously when we come home from work. Our nanny says she rarely whines during the day. What's really upsetting me is that my husband absolutely hates the whining and gets angry at me for letting her whine. Please help.

Your husband and you need to decide either to ignore your daughter's whining or call a time-out each time she whines. What's most important is that you both agree on how you handle the whining. The discussion and argument that result each time your daughter whines is actually encouraging her to whine more. Although it isn't absolutely clear why parents' differences worsen childern's behaviors, they always do. If you support each other, with patience and consistency your daughter's whining will gradually disappear.

Boy Prefers Mom

My four-year-old son frequently wants me to do things for him, but he won't let his father help him. He even tells his dad he hates him. My husband feels terrible about this. I feel we should ignore it, but my husband worries he is doing something wrong.

This problem can really feed on itself if you let things get out of hand. However, just a few changes in you and your husband's behavior might shape things right up.

First, it's important that you don't intervene. When your son refuses his father's help and comes to you for assistance, you can slip out of the room or say, "I'm busy, your daddy can help you." Your husband should stand his ground and insist on helping him (unless it's something your son can do by himself). Your husband should ignore the "I hate you" comments that your son makes. Eventually, your son will realize that this comment doesn't elicit a response, and he will stop saying it. Actually, he'll probably not say it at all if he believes you're nowhere around. He's only hoping to get your attention.

You might also encourage your son and your husband to spend some time alone with each other. They might plan a special activity or start a new project in order to strengthen their relationship. If your husband teaches your child a new skill that he enjoys, he might realize that his dad is there as a helper and a teacher. He'll soon become more enthusiastic about coming to his dad for help.

10

Finding Good Day Care for Your Preschooler

Aa Bb Cc Dd   Ff Gg Hh

Y ou may be looking for day care as a part-time opportunity for your children or as a requirement to allow you to work full time outside your home. The criteria are surprisingly similar, except that consistency and communication between home and school are even more critical if your children will spend a fair amount of their day away from home. The communication between school and home is important not only because you will feel more secure about the environment that is being provided for your children, but also because you, as parents, can share in your children's development and milestones despite not being able to be with them much of the time. Chapter 11 includes more on communication.

You will want to visit and observe a day-care center or pre-school that you are considering for your children. A list of criteria to consider follows and a sample checklist for evaluating a facility can be found later in this chapter.

Atmosphere

Child-care providers should be loving toward all the children. If staff members seem to be targeting some children as troublemakers in their conversations, consider that your children could become one of those children, and that would not be a good school start. If instead they emphasize positive approaches to behavior problems, you can anticipate a more supportive environment for your children.

Staff

You will first want to notice the staff-to-child ratio. Ideally, there should be no more than eight children to one staff member. For younger children, the ratio should be 4:1 or 6:1, depending on the ages of the preschoolers.

Ask about the education and training of the staff. The director should at least have a college degree in the area of preschool education. Other staff members may have participated in two-year programs and should be involved in regular in-service training.

Stability is also important. Schools that have a history of high staff turnover may either not be selecting staff well or not training them sufficiently. It is also possible that the leadership of the school is inadequate. Obviously, occasional changes of staff are normal. You can obtain that information best from other parents who had children at the school. If teachers have left with frequency, you may also want to find out the reason. If your children need to adjust to continual changes in staff, it could cause them unnecessary stress. Furthermore, high staff turnover may cause inconsistency in teaching approaches and programs.

Classroom Organization

Reasonable organization and limit setting are critical for children's early learning of responsibility and self-discipline. Routines that teach children good manners, cleanup responsibilities, consideration for others, and respect for teachers in charge provide good preparation for school. Disorganized, out-of-control class environments will cause feelings of insecurity for your children, which will be observable when they are at home. Rigid control in day care can also be a problem, although that's found less often if teachers are knowledgeable about the development and needs of preschoolers.

Fostering the Love of Books

Most day-care centers and preschools foster the love of books, since reading is a prerequisite of the love of learning. Several story hours a day should not be replaced by a convenient television set, and television should either make up a very small part of children's learning in preschool or not be present at all.

Art, Creative Expression, and Curiosity

Toys and equipment should include painting and drawing supplies, puzzles, small and large building blocks, pretend and imagination toys, as well as sturdy outdoor equipment. An atmosphere in which children are expected to explore, to create and invent and feel and touch rather than copy adult direction, filling lines on work pages, underscores a creative environment. Observe to determine if children's curiosity is encouraged. If the structure is too rigid, their interests will be stifled.

Music, Dance, and Movement

Creative movement provides opportunities for the development of children's love of music and rhythm. Dance or some form of movement to music should be part of almost every preschool day. Music has also been found to be important for early brain development.

Outdoor Play and Exploration

The exploration of nature may be limited in urban centers, but learning about weather, animals, and nature can be carried out at parks and playgrounds and is important for children. Observation skills and curiosity are encouraged by an awareness of the outdoors. Environmental awareness is important even at preschool age.

Academic Preparation

Preschool should provide some academic preparation, but not too much. A more holistic approach is important for children to develop appropriately. By age four, more academic preparation begins to be introduced.

Value Systems

Religious points of view, values about honesty, respect, animal life, conservation, etc., should be reasonable matches with your family values. Although they need not be identical, they should at least be complementary to what you believe is appropriate for your children.

Freedom to Choose Within Limitations

Some school curriculums are the same for the whole class, and others permit children to make all the choices based on their interests and development. Rigid preschool lessons will not tap individual differences. Allowing the children to make all the choices of activities is also risky. Children are likely to select their areas of interest and pursue them, but may ignore or neglect some of the more boring skills they may require for kindergarten. Furthermore, a school that permits children to make all the choices empowers preschoolers too much. The children may assume school will always be that way and balk at later school environments that feel restrictive by comparison.

Nutrition

If your child will be eating breakfast or lunch at the day-care center, ask about the nutritional program and alternatives for food. Hot lunches can be very nice for a two-career family that doesn't have time to prepare a hot meal in the evening. On the other hand, you may wish to send sandwiches or snacks to school that you know your children will eat if they are fussy eaters—although fussy eaters sometimes become less fussy when they eat with a group.

Naps

Check to see how the center's nap schedule fits with your children's present routine. You may need to make some changes in your child's routine if there are problems, or you may want to ask the center to make adjustments for your child. Related questions and discussions can help you assess the flexibility of the staff. Preschool children do require adjustments, particularly before they learn the routines of the school. An early riser may need some morning and afternoon rest time, which is probably routine, but asking about eating and sleeping information will be reassuring and will also help you determine if you should change your child's bedtime.

Firsthand observations of a preschool class in session, using a checklist and making notes, will help you to evaluate these criteria and some personal issues of your own. An interview with the teacher and some telephone calls to other parents will assist in gathering information. Sifting through your information with consideration for your personal priorities will lead you to comfortable decision making.

If you have already placed your child in day care and want to observe to see how it's going, watch both your child and another child in the classroom. If the teacher knows you are watching her interaction with your child, she will treat your child differently. Your noticing how she treats other children will give you a more accurate picture of how she typically treats your child.

Alternative Child-Care Providers

If you plan to have a child-care provider, nanny, or relative care for your children in your own home, a visit to a good preschool will provide you with ideas to share with that person. The checklist in this chapter for selecting a day-care center can also be used for interviewing a child-care provider. Chapter 11, on communication, will provide further suggestions for ways you can stay in close touch with your child who is being cared for by another person.

Selecting a Child-Care Provider

Selection of a good child-care provider can be more difficult than choosing a day-care center. If there is an agency in your community that provides thorough screening or training, it may be helpful. You may find these agencies listed in your Yellow Pages under Child Care or Child Care Referral Services. Interview the agency director first to familiarize yourself with the screening process so that you can be assured that your children will be safe and well cared for. Afterward, you should also have the opportunity to thoroughly interview the child-care provider. Be certain that the agency provides for a trial period. You should never feel obligated to keep a child-care provider whom you believe might not be appropriate. Your child-care provider will have a dramatic influence on your children.

A referral from a friend or an advertisement in the newspaper may also be a source for finding child-care providers. In either case, you will want to check references carefully and interview thoroughly. If possible, invite the caretaker to your home to care for your children for several hours while you are there so you can observe the interactions between adult and children. Although you are observing them at their best because they know you are watching, at least you can see what their best is like.

Relatives

If relatives are helping you care for your children, it's a good idea to provide written guidelines for their use. It is terribly easy to offend a person you love by telling them how you'd like your child cared for when they are in fact doing you a great favor and believe themselves to be qualified and experienced. If you can informally explain that you thought it would be helpful to everyone for you to write down guidelines, at least your family caretaker will have exposure to your most important principals. They'll undoubtedly do some things differently than you would, but they should as least respect your most important concerns.

If you're unhappy with the way a relative is caring for your children, relationships may become strained. If you have any other choice, and you are truly unhappy with their child-care approach, take the courage to move your children elsewhere, despite the fact you may be hurting that relative's feelings. Of course, that doesn't mean the loving relative wouldn't see the child after that, only that she wouldn't have such complete care and influence. If you have no choice, and many parents don't, be as instructive and supportive as possible.

Home Child Care

The most frequent kind of care for children is in someone's home with a parent or other adult who is taking care of several preschoolers. Although this may seem like the best kind of care for your children at first because of its homey atmosphere, it is only as good as the child-care provider. It will give you important information if you can observe her approach with her own children in her home. Your day-care checklist (below) will also be helpful as you ask the day-care provider about her choices for activities for children. Be sure to ask which television programs she permits the children to watch. Notice the language she uses when talking to the children. Your children will be learning many of their first verbal skills through your child-care provider. Even the general mood of the home provides an important influence for your children. If the atmosphere is not positive, it can have a seriously adverse effect on your child.

Realism

Although I've suggested you look for an optimal child-care environment, I recognize that economy and necessity will be an important part of your decision making, and you may need to make some compromises with the high standards you prefer. I hope this and the preceding chapter will help you think through your decisions carefully so you can select the best possible environment for your children.

Checklist for Evaluating Day Care

	EXCELLENT	GOOD	FAIR	POOR
Atmosphere	____	____	____	____
Staff-Student Ratio	____	____	____	____
Education and Training of Staff	____	____	____	____
Stability of Staff	____	____	____	____
Classroom Organization	____	____	____	____
Foster Love of Books	____	____	____	____
Art, Creative Expression	____	____	____	____
Music, Dance Movement	____	____	____	____
Outdoor Play, Exploration	____	____	____	____
Academic Preparation	____	____	____	____
Value System	____	____	____	____
Freedom of Choices	____	____	____	____
Nutrition	____	____	____	____
Naps	____	____	____	____

Notes: _____

_____

_____

_____

Summary Advice

- Use the day-care checklist for evaluating preschools and day care.
- Check references thoroughly.
- Observe interactions with children.
- Notice child-care provider's use of language.
- Find a positive atmosphere.
- Be willing to make some compromises.

Girl Not Assertive

I've been researching the subject of assertiveness in children in order to help my two-and-a-half-year-old daughter but have found nothing helpful for our situation.

My daughter does not go to day care, and she is an only child, so far. The problem is that when we are around other children and they take toys away from her, she lets them, and then comes crying to me that she wants them back. I've talked with her and told her to hold on tight to the toy if she doesn't want it taken from her. I've also told her to tell the child, "Stop, don't take my toy." She can play with it awhile and then take turns.

She tried the holding-on-tight method, but when the child started crying, she became upset, gave her the toy, and came to me crying that she wanted it back. I told her if she wanted it, she shouldn't have given it away.

Also, if a child hits her, bites her, or kicks her, and the parent disciplines the child, my daughter will go and pat the child and tell them it's okay.

She'll be going to preschool soon, and I'm afraid for her. Any suggestions?

At least you can be pleased your daughter isn't too aggressive, which would cause you and her more of a problem. At age two and a half, most children are not very verbal and they are concrete in their thinking, so your advice about holding on and taking turns is appropriate. It's all right for Mom to intervene at this age to explain to two children what taking turns means. You can even use a timer to help children understand when they should give a toy to the other child if the child continues to want it. While one child plays with the toy, distract the other by giving her something else to play with while she's waiting. By the time the buzzer goes off, the other child may no longer want the first toy. Gradually, the children will learn to share.

As to your daughter's kindness after being hurt, forgiveness is a wonderful quality. After all, the child who hit her is only a toddler and deserves only a reprimand until she learns.

Of course, you want your daughter to grow to be both resilient and assertive. Her confidence can grow gradually in many ways as she learns social skills. Because I've observed so many aggressive children recently who, in the name of assertiveness, haven't learned to respect others, I would encourage you to be thankful for your sweet little daughter. Her first years of preschool will teach her many social lessons, but she's had a good start in learning to share.

Signs of Readiness for Preschool

We've planned for our three-year-old to start preschool. We believe she's ready. I've worked with her on many similar skills she'd be doing at preschool. What signs or behaviors will tell us she's not ready when she begins?

Three-year-olds are always ready to attend preschool, provided the program is geared to their developmental needs. If the program has mixed ages with your child being the youngest, there could be problems. Look for signs of tension, such as more than usual thumb sucking, whining, crying, not sleeping at night, or regression in toilet training.

A full-day preschool environment for three-year-olds usually includes an afternoon nap, which children that age typically require to get through a whole day. Also, a three-year-old program should include music, play, rhythms, stories, but very few academic skills.

Be sure to allow at least a month for adjustment. Many children show initial symptoms of stress at separation from their mommies, but as they accustom themselves to their caring teachers, the symptoms disappear. If you are concerned about your daughter's adjustment, talk to her teacher; they may have ideas for helping her.

Effects of Grandmother's Leaving on Child

My wife and I are the proud parents of a beautiful, healthy, and well-adjusted sixteen-month-old baby boy. My wife is European and her mother has been living with us for the last six months. She is a very warm and loving person and has helped with day care while my wife works three days per week. Needless to say, she and the boy have become very close, and I know he loves her as he loves my wife and me.

I am troubled because my mother-in-law must return to her life in Europe next month. I'm sure this will have a negative effect on all of us, but I'm really concerned about the baby. Will he be emotionally scarred from this? What can we do to minimize his trauma when he realizes she is gone?

He will probably spend one day per week with my parents, whom he also loves, but I am fearful that the other two days in day care will only exacerbate any insecurities he would have about her suddenly being gone from his life.

You can cheer up with confidence. Although the relationship was surely good for your son, the adults will probably suffer more pain than him. Within a few days your son will not remember his grandmother except subconsciously, unless you continue to talk aloud about her and show him pictures. Even that will not cause him to be unhappy. Although he may miss her temporarily and even be happy to see her if you keep her fresh in his mind by your reminders, he will definitely not be emotionally scarred unless his day care is inadequate. You can dissipate any trauma by deciding to provide loving care for your son. That is not always easy in a day-care environment, so choose carefully. There are many wonderful people to love your son temporarily, but your permanent love is most important to him.

A Boy and a Girl Unhappy at Preschool

My four-year-old son started preschool in January. He was very excited about school, and his first day at school went fine. On his second day, another boy pulled his pants down and laughed at him. I talked to the teacher and the director about this. It has been a nightmare ever since. He complains about hating school and does not want to go even though he has a great time when he is there. When I want to leave

*for work he starts crying and clinging to my leg. We have to get the
teachers to restrain him so he doesn't run after me. At home he is a
typical little boy, yet at school he acts wimpy, talks like a baby, and the
teachers have to encourage him to get involved because he is so shy.*

*Should I discontinue taking him to school? Am I doing more
damage by making him go? Do you think the day is too long or he
is too young? Is this a power play for him to see how much control
he has and to get his own way? Should I give him more time to get
used to going to school? He attends two days while most of the children attend full time.*

*My three-and-a-half-year-old daughter has a difficult time going to
day care, although she has been in a day-care center practically full
time since she was four months old.*

*My husband and I have made many changes to our schedules to
encourage her. Despite all of our efforts to be cheerful and positively discuss the events she has to look forward to throughout the
day and in the evening, she still gets anxious when we attempt to
leave the center. Getting her there before any of the other children
arrive seems to help, and, of course, we help her with her outerwear
and get her cubby squared away, sometimes even staying to work a
puzzle with her to get her involved with a toy or with her favorite
caregiver. Even so, she frequently begins to cry and has actually
thrown tantrums. The center is the only one in my rural area, and I
think it is a good one. The staff has tried to help, and they report that
she gets over it soon after we leave.*

I can assure both of you that you are not the only mothers who
are in the dilemma of watching your children cry as you leave
them at a day-care center. Positive, matter-of-fact attitudes are
your best allies. Don't stay with the children to play or dress them.
They will only cry or lose their tempers while you're present because they continue to hope they can keep you there as long as
they can see you. Once you have absented yourself, your children
will know that their crying won't help, and they'll soon settle down
and play with their classmates until you return.

Three- and four-year-olds are not too young for preschool. If
you pull them out now, you may face an exaggerated form of the
problem, school phobia, by the time they attend kindergarten.

While it is important to persevere, you will also want to receive
daily feedback from the teachers so that you have confidence that

your children's behavior is improving. You will want to ask the teachers if they notice other children who may be teasing or berating your children. You've both commented on the good quality of the schools, or I would certainly suggest that you confirm that quality by observing and by talking to other parents.

Try not to talk about the issue to other adults within your children's hearing (referential speaking). If your children believe that you consider it to be a major problem, they will feel more anxious. If you are matter-of-fact, they will soon accept and adjust. A sticker on the kitchen calendar for each happy day they have at day care may speed up the adjustment and make a fun game out of the situation.

Child Not Adjusting to Day Care

I have my eighteen-month-old son in an in-home day care two days a week. The caregiver also watches three other children (ten months, eighteen months, and two-and-a-half years). My son has been in the sitter's care for over a month now and is still not adjusting well. I pack his favorite stuffed animal, blanket, and cup with him. He cries most of the day and is not content unless he is on the sitter's lap (where he spends most of the day). The first week he refused to eat or drink all day. Although now he is eating and drinking, he still does not socialize or play.

At home, my husband and I have been trying to encourage our son's independence by "making" him play by himself in another room for ten minutes at a time. That is not going well, either. We were hoping this would help him at day care. Is it going to help? What can we do and what can the sitter do to help him adjust? We are changing sitters now; my current sitter has run out of patience. With another baby on the way, we can't afford to lose my part-time income now. Please offer some advice.

Your son moved from an environment of no children to being one of four. Although such an adjustment goes smoothly for many children, separation is more difficult for some. The fact that your son's now eating and drinking normally shows a beginning of adjustment. It's too bad the sitter didn't insist on putting him down to play with the other children. I think he would have adjusted sooner.

If the sitter prefers not to keep your son, perhaps it's better that he not stay with her, although a change to another child-care provider will mean further adjustment. Your new child-care person should not hold him continuously, but can try helping him to learn to play alongside of other children who may be there. If the caregiver is experienced, this transition may be better.

It is good to let a toddler play alone in a safe place for a few minutes each day. You may want to leave some toys or cloth books in your son's crib for him to play with when he awakens. Even when you and your husband are in the same room with him, if you read or busy yourselves with your own activities and occasionally introduce a different toy, you'll find your son can entertain himself more and more. Of course, some interactive play and talk are important for your son's intellectual, emotional, and social development, but an eighteen-month-old child should not need to be held all day. The tears will stop after a little time and distraction. Hope that the next adjustment will be much faster.

11

Communication with Your Child-Care Providers

W hether you have a baby-sitter in your home to care for your children when you're out for a few hours, or whether you have full-time day care, good communication is the foundation of appropriate care. It is most important that parents make their parenting style known to those whom they pay to care for their children and that they respect the professionalism or knowledge that the caregiver brings to the position. That is always a delicate balance. The child-care provider's personality, rather than knowledge, may have much to do with communication. Sometimes parents feel so intimidated by the child-care provider that they fear giving input. Other times they give so much advice that they intimidate the child-care provider, and the provider becomes fearful about independent decision making. Either extreme is not typical, but your awareness of those possibilities is important.

Baby-sitters

For a baby-sitter who is coming only for an evening, you will want to prepare a written list of routines and emergency numbers. These can be posted on the refrigerator or other convenient place. If this is the first time for your baby-sitter, review the list with her or him orally, and ask if there are any further questions. Also review any general routines and take the sitter on a tour of your home so they become familiar with the locations of each child's room. If there are a few tricks your children like to play on a new sitter, like "Mom always reads us ten stories" or "We're always allowed to have chocolate before bedtime," you will want to remind your children and the baby-sitter of the number of books and the appropriate snack foods you typically give your children. Your written guidelines will also help your baby-sitter to enforce your rules. She can say, "Mom said seven o'clock," if your children should be determined to push their bedtime.

It's always important that the sitter knows where to contact you if there is an emergency. That reminder needs to be given each time a sitter comes, even if the sitter has been there many times. It's also important to review the place where you keep your list of routines and telephone numbers—even an experienced baby-sitter could forget. See the facing page for a sample of baby-sitter instructions.

Leave your children with positive hugs and kisses and don't tarry if there are a few tears. The tears usually disappear before you've driven down the driveway. That holds true for extreme crying as well, but if this is a new baby-sitter or the tears suggest some major unsuspected problems, reassurances or investigation may be appropriate. Parents do always need to be alert to potential problems, but if you have confidence in your child-care provider— and you should not have caregivers you don't have confidence in—parting tears may only represent a stage in your child's development. If you're worried when you leave, a telephone call to the sitter fifteen minutes later may reassure you without further arousing your children. Because you have left your number, you may not even need to call. No news is good news!

BABY-SITTING INFORMATION FOR JARED AND SAMANTHA RONE

ADDRESS: 29 Oak Tree Drive East, Northwalk, CT 08650
Directions: I-95 to exit 59. Off exit ramp, take a right turn onto
Thorn Apple Way toward Woodbine Road. Go 0.5 mi., turn right on
Windward Road (next to church). Follow Windward to bottom of hill
(.3 mi.) onto Oak Tree Drive East. House is at the end of the cul-
de-sac, blue with black shutters.
HOME TELEPHONE NO.: 203-401-7212
PARENTS: Mark and Michelle Rone

PERMANENT CONTACT TELEPHONE #'S
Mary Randall (Michelle's mother): 216-459-9232, Ohio
Bernard & Sandy Rone (Mark's parents): 414-261-6243, Wisconsin

EMERGENCY CONTACTS
Mark's Work #'s: Office, 797-4326; Lab: 797-4327; Cytology: 796-
   3540; Beeper: 566-0321 (after beep, enter your telephone #)
Michelle's Work #: 796-5009
Linda and Tom Vincent (neighbors, 32 Oak Tree), 401-4551
Susan and Ed Epstein (3 houses away, 38 Oak Tree), 401-2352
Other emergency #'s: 911

CHILDREN'S PERSONAL INFORMATION
Jared Adam Rone
Birthdate: 1/21/91
SS#: 044-91-7170
Allergies/Medical Problems: None Known

Samantha Lynn Rone
Birthdate: 7/9/92
SS#: 043-90-5804
Allergies/Medical Problems: None Known

MEDICAL INFO
Connecticut Health Plan (Main provider #478-33-7321)
Pediatrician: John O'Donnell, M.D. 433-1578
Weekend/evening: 433-2326

MEALS/EATING: May have snacks (found in cupboard or refrigerator) but *must* be sitting at table in kitchen or on deck (in nice
weather) when eating. May not carry food or cups around house.
Occasionally may have popcorn, etc., in family room while watching
movie.

PLAYING: There are lots of toys and books in each of their rooms and the basement playroom. We try to keep most playing centered in these areas. The bins of toys in the garage (balls, skates, etc.) are "outside toys" and are not to be used in the house. The kids are allowed to ride bikes, draw with chalk, etc, in the cul-de-sac but must be accompanied by an adult at all times. The kids should help to put toys away before going to bed.

TV/VIDEO: Appropriate television or various kid videotapes may be watched on request and with parents' permission (check with us beforehand on all TV use). No more than one half hour a day. Baby-sitters may use the TV and VCR after children are in bed.

BEDTIME: Kids are to be in pajamas by 8:00, brush teeth, must go to the bathroom, can read books, and in bed by 8:15. May have a cup of water beside bed; may not get up and down after in bed unless coughing or sick, etc. May have books, stuffed animals, or a toy in bed with them. Once in bed, may have night-light turned on, bedroom door open, and bathroom light on; may not get out of bed unless it is to use the bathroom.

WHERE WE'LL BE: _____

_____

BE SURE YOU HAVE FUN, FUN, FUN!!

Courtesy of Janet Rimm

Other Child-Care Providers

Your child-care provider requires team support. If you disagree with an approach she uses, discuss your differences outside your children's hearing. If your children hear about your disagreement, they are likely to become disrespectful either to your child-care provider or to you or your spouse. Team cooperation is important for effective child care.

If your children attend day care, the day-care center probably has a formal method of communication. Ask about the possibility of sending notes back and forth. There is probably little time at drop-off or pickup times for much oral communication. There may be opportunities for telephone conversations at specified times, and they can be effective and private.

After Divorce

Communication after divorce is probably most complex for parents and child-care providers. It is best that two copies of all written communication be available for both custodial parents if there is joint custody. Parents should provide a written schedule to the day-care center or provider of who will be dropping and picking up children. Clear communication under these special circumstances is critical.

Journals

Communication with a nanny or all-day home provider should include not only a schedule and list of emergency numbers but should involve a two-way journal. Sample entries in a nanny's journal are shown below. Your child-care provider can list the cute new things your child is doing, activities, new words, play interactions with other children, television viewing or computer use, your child's daily diet, nap schedules, and descriptions of behaviors. Your child-care provider should also note any questions for you, even if she intends to ask them orally. You should review the journal each day and add comments, ask questions, and note any changes in schedule in the evening that could affect your child the next day. This also provides an opportunity to make suggestions in an unobtrusive way whether or not you have time to discuss questions before you leave for work. The journal serves as a nice memory book for you as well, but most important, it keeps you in touch with your child's progress and gives you input. It also causes your day-care provider to feel more accountable and to know that you care about the quality of her caretaking. A caregiver from another country will in addition be provided with an excellent opportunity to practice her written English in a journal.

A few minutes for oral communication when your child-care provider arrives and leaves is also important, even if your words only review what has already been written. If you have a relative who is volunteering her time for child care or doing it for little money, she may be less willing to write in a journal, but notes back and forth are still important. Using a regular notebook for those notes can provide a collection of information that is similar to a

Samples of Journal Entries

October 27, 1996

Miriam had a very happy day! We played in Ben's room with the puppets. Miriam suggested we have a puppet show about a bunny and a farmer. Miriam said, "The bunny is usually the bad one, so I'll be the bunny because I know how to be bad sometimes!" It was funny.

Miriam was dressed extremely fast today. She is really becoming such a big girl!

Miriam and I listened to Ben talk, talk, talk on the way to school. Miriam said, "Ben is *certainly* learning how to talk!!" "What does certainly mean?" It was funny.

January 25, 1997

Ben had a happy, fun day today. After Mommy left for work, Ben spent some time in his room because he didn't want to finish his milk, but after two times back and forth, he decided to sit down like a big boy and finish *all* of his breakfast!

He played in his toy car and had a ball, as usual. He said, "I broke a door. I hafta climb out a window!" He tried it once and fell down and decided he didn't like that, so he said, "I fix a door; all better!" He is a silly boy!

Ben was a big help to me today with the laundry. "Oooh, these pants are mine," "Oooh, this shirt . . ." All of a sudden he said, "I think I hafta go potty!" He made pee-pee in the potty and sat for about fifteen minutes and did make a big poopie. He's getting there! So, off we were to put on big-boy underwear. He said, "Oooh, I like this. I hafta tell Daddy about this!"

He played in his bed with his Matchbox cars until it was time to take Miriam to school. He tried to put on his mittens by himself, but he was quickly frustrated. "I can't do it; it's hard. Help me, please. I don't like this mitten."

Courtesy of Ilonna Rimm, Joseph Madsen, and their children's nanny, Eileen Ihm journal. You may wish to spend more time on oral communication because less is written.

Private Communication

It's probably a good idea to manage a little private time for communication with your baby-sitter during which your children can't hear you talk about anything that they shouldn't hear. If this isn't possible because the children are too young to leave alone for even a few minutes, written notes are especially important, or you may wish to arrange for telephone communication later if an important message needs to be shared privately. If Rob constantly hears about how he picks on his sister, you can almost count on that behavior growing worse. Referential speaking, or talk between adults within children's hearing, can have powerful positive or negative effects. Like direct praise or put-downs, it sets expectations for your children and reinforces either positive or negative behaviors. Referential talk between you and your child-care provider can be used purposefully to encourage your children's appropriate behavior, but negative referential talk can cause major problems for your children and should be monitored carefully. Parents may wish to specifically review this policy with all providers of care for their children.

Summary Advice

- Provide clear written guidelines for your child-care provider.
- Include activities, values, and discipline.
- Encourage oral and written communication about your child.
- Support your child-care provider.
- Be mindful of referential speaking.

Stressed Preschooler in Day Care

My son, Scott, is three years old. He started going to day care for the first time. He seemed to be adjusting really well at first. Then we started getting notes from his teacher that he was having problems. A few days later there was a problem with Scott wetting his pants, or getting to the toilet but wetting on the floor. Before this, Scott never had any of these problems at home. Now, we are receiving letters stating he needs to work on his motor skills and that he's to be careful when he colors and that I need to teach him how to scribble and how to hold the crayon correctly. To me this all seems to be too much pressure on Scott. If the teacher puts stress on him in day care and he comes home and I continue to put stress on him some more, how good can this be for him? Do you have any advice on this for me?

It does indeed seem that your son is showing symptoms of stress. You mentioned his wetting his pants, but you didn't say whether he seems happy to go to day care or is happily playing when you pick him up. Sometimes children show symptoms of stress when they first adjust to a new environment, but the symptoms go away after a few weeks.

The activities of a three-year-old's day-care program usually include group play, singing, listening to stories, and small muscle coordination tasks such as working with crayons (mainly scribbling) or painting on an easel. Social skills, such as taking turns and sharing, are typically important. It should not put pressure on your son if you encourage him to draw or scribble with "fat" crayons. He can even tell you little stories about his pictures, but I promise you that Scott's scribbles are not likely to look much like artwork.

I would suggest that you ask his teacher if you may observe your son in day care. You'll readily be able to see if he fits in well with the other children. You might also want to see if he is in a mixed-age class and if your son is expected to keep up with four- and five-year-olds. If it is a good day-care center, that's unlikely. You will want to notice if the teachers are patient and calm with the children. You may feel reassured after watching him with other children.

If you feel less anxious, Scott may also feel better, and after a few weeks, may adjust quite nicely. However, if your observation of the school suggests that it sets too high expectations for your son, take him out and either look for a less pressured nursery school or consider forming a play group with a few friends who have children of similar age. You and your friends can rotate providing leadership and teaching the children to play together. However, you too will probably want to include in your activities simple tasks to develop Scott's small muscle coordination, including "scribbling" pretty pictures.

12

When a New Baby Comes

Your little boy is five years old (or three or four). This happy, pleasant, verbal little guy has been the center of everyone's attention. Grandmom even calls him "the little king."

There is good news ahead. You and your husband are bursting with joy. Your son will soon have a little sister. You can't wait to share all the details with the big brother-to-be. Yet, you're not sure when or what to tell him. Finally, you get the courage.

"Jason," you exclaim excitedly, "I know you're going to love this good news. Mommy and Daddy are going to have a baby!"

You're enthusiastic, but alas Jason doesn't even seem to care. He leaves the room and runs to play on his swing set. You follow him to explain further. You continue to talk enthusiastically, and he seems bored. Finally, he asks when the baby's coming. You respond, "In April." Jason says, "April, that's far away. Is that after my birthday?" Jason runs to the climbing bars, apparently totally unconcerned about the conversation.

Preschool children think concretely. They don't see a baby; the future is far away, and they're busy playing happily in, you hope, a secure world. Gradually, as the time gets nearer and the baby becomes more apparent, Jason will ask more questions and even become a little more interested.

Jason won't even notice as the baby increases in size. As you arrive at your last three months, you may wish to let Jason feel his baby brother or sister kicking. Most mothers refer to the baby as being in their "tummy" and that probably won't cause any real problems. You may wish to explain that the baby is in a special room inside Mommy called a "womb." Either way, Jason may ask how the baby can grow there and how it will come out. You can explain that the baby is protected and safe within the womb and is getting its food through you, and when it's ready to come out, there is a special opening for it to come through. Don't be surprised or disappointed if you don't get even that many questions, but your Jason may surprise you with a few you hadn't thought of. Answer them simply, because your child is usually thinking simply.

A few weeks before the baby arrives, be sure to read some books about new brothers and sisters to your children. Let them help decorate the room and get things ready if you're getting things ready. If you're not because you prefer to wait until later, your children don't require the readiness so much as they need the involvement with you.

When Baby Comes

When the new baby comes, the feelings and the questions are quite different, and the feelings children have aren't often expressed well. They always miss their mother when they go to the hospital, and when the baby comes home, they *always* miss parental attention. Although parents may feel tired after the new baby arrives at home, be sure that both Mom and Dad find some one-to-one time for the older siblings. Also, older children can have special tasks, like bringing diapers when you require them or bringing a toy to be placed in the baby's cradle or crib. They may also want to get the baby a special gift of their own.

Many gifts will arrive for the new baby, and you may worry about your older children feeling jealous. Sometimes friends will bring them a gift as well, but many won't. You can explain that to your older children by comparing it to a birthday. Little sister or brother won't get many gifts on Jason's birthday, either. Jason can help unwrap the baby's gifts and even thank the friends on behalf of the baby. Jason will like the idea of talking for the baby until the baby is old enough to talk on her own.

Family and friends will want to welcome the new baby and a great deal of company will be stopping by. There will be plenty of "The baby looks just like Grandma" comments. Of course, conversation will center on the baby. Add a few positive comments about Jason from time to time. Be sure to refer to the good big brother he's becoming and how gentle and kind he is to his new sister. Hearing those comments about himself will encourage kindness and help him to share attention.

Symptoms of Sibling Rivalry

Some first children feel very jealous and express it immediately in mean or aggressive things they do to others and even to the baby. If indeed there are a few aggressive behaviors, be clear and firm that these aren't acceptable, but don't discuss with other adults the new negative behaviors within Jason's hearing, or you will see the behaviors increase.

Sometimes older siblings regress and ask for baby toys and baby bottles. They may even wet their pants or their beds. More, however, seem content, happy, and excited about the new baby and express their feelings of sibling rivalry much later, when the baby is a year old, begins walking, or, especially, when the baby is old enough to grab their toys. Eventually, children learn to share attention, but some sibling rivalry is natural.

Summary Advice

- Read stories about new brothers and sisters a month before the baby comes.
- Let older children help prepare for the baby's arrival.
- Permit older children to choose a special gift for the baby.

(*continued*)

- Be sure to find special one-to-one time for older children.
- Assign older children helping jobs and let them know you appreciate the help.
- Don't focus all your conversation on the new baby.
- Casually mention to other adults, within the older child's earshot, what a gentle big brother (sister) he (she) is.
- If the older sibling is aggressive toward the baby, don't chat about it to other adults within your child's hearing.

Girl Cries Easily

My four-and-a-half-year-old daughter cries really easily over the slightest thing. I would like to teach her how to express herself in words instead of crying, especially before she goes to kindergarten.

I would guess that your four-and-a-half-year-old has a new baby in the household, because that is a frequent reason for more than typical crying. Whether or not that is true, my suggestions are fairly similar. Be sure your daughter gets some one-to-one attention each day so that she doesn't feel like her sibling is getting it all. Absolutely never give her what she wants if crying is her way of communicating with you. Give her a warning by saying, "Use words," but if she continues to whine and cry, tell her to go to her room until she feels ready to communicate in words.

It's difficult to be consistent when the crying is so persistent and annoying. However, if you can manage to give her the choice of speaking or going to her room each time she cries, she'll quickly get out of her bad habit.

Incidentally, there probably is no worry about her crying in school. Peer pressure usually prevents too many tears. I'm assuming that her tears simply have been effective for getting her what she wants. If there are issues, like illness or major disruptions at home, then the tears will need to be handled much differently.

13

Sibling Rivalry

Sibling rivalry is normal when not extreme. In order not to exacerbate it, don't try to treat children equally, only fairly. Sibling rivalry is not likely ever to be eliminated, nor should it be. If there are no brother-sister struggles in a family, parents should assume that one child is giving orders and the other is accepting those orders. Children should have differences and should be assertive enough to express and even argue those differences. Thus, some sibling quarrels and fights are a healthy indication that none of the children are completely submissive. Part of your children's experiences involve learning to solve problems when there are differences.

When preschool children fight or grab one another's toys, parents and teachers need to explain with simple, concrete statements. Cue words like "share," "take turns," or "be gentle" are often effective in quickly changing their behavior. Explanations such as "How would you feel if Danny did this to you?" fall on deaf ears at this age. Even if they know the correct answer to your question, they are not yet able to understand empathy.

The oldest child is usually hardest on the next in birth order and on down the line. Children one and three, two and four, etc., tend to have closer relationships. Same-gender children close in age often show more rivalry, perhaps because they have more similarities.

Don't be surprised if your children display opposite characteristics. If one child is tidy, the other is more likely to be sloppy. If one is aggressive, the other is more likely to be submissive. Although some of these differences may be related to inherited temperaments, the pervasiveness of these differences suggests that they are more related to the children's competition for parental attention and finding their special niche. Don't compare your children within their hearing. It's almost impossible not to make any comparisons when you're talking privately, so don't feel guilty about those.

Secrets and Surprises

Helping children plan surprises builds cooperative feelings and behaviors. When one parent gets the children together to plan a surprise for the other parent or for another child, then the children get involved in cooperative planning and feel closer. An alliance with a positive goal builds unity. The secrets of gift giving, surprises, concerts, performances, and parties for Mother's Day, Father's Day, Christmas, birthdays, or just for company seem to unite brothers and sisters and diminish arguing. You can always add a few extra secrets if grandparents or aunts and uncles are planning visits.

Building Cooperative Relationships

A point system can be used temporarily to reward your children for their being nice to each other. This works particularly well when your children are required to spend a great amount of time together; for example, on a long car ride. You may wish to put stars on a chart for every half hour of peace and kindness. Ten stars could mean a special ice cream treat, which kids will definitely enjoy after a long car ride. No system works for long, but it will be effective at particularly stressful times.

Setting Limits

Although parents do need to teach preschool children the art of being nice to each other, be careful you don't always side with the younger child or blame the older one, or the younger one may begin the habit of trapping the older one by teasing. Sometimes children argue and fight just to get parental attention. If that seems to be happening, instead of discussing every argument, use the "time-away" approach. Reserve the option of separating your children for fifteen minutes or a half hour. Any two different rooms will do. Plan the rooms ahead of time, or your children will argue about which room to go to. You'll find your children love to play with each other so much that separating them for a little while will encourage peace more than your interventions and negative attention.

Do set a limit for a reasonable noise level or aggressive behavior. If your children put each other down, don't take sides at the time. However, you should communicate your concern privately to the one who is doing the putting down. Tell the child you'll be noticing his or her efforts and will give a secret signal when you notice that they are nice. Give the child the appropriate words for nice talk like "You're my friend," "I like you," or "Would you like to play with my truck?" Positive secret signals are amazingly effective. You can use cue words as signals like, "It's a sunny day," or you can touch your ear or your child's shoulder to let the child know you've noticed the good behavior.

A parent team helps to minimize sibling competition. If parents support each other, children will be less likely to take sides with one parent against the other, and vice versa. Here's a comical example: At a recent talk to parents, during a question and answer session, I received the following question from a mother: "My three preschool children seem to show extreme sibling rivalry, even compared to what I see in other families. They argue constantly. Do you have any suggestions?" I posed several possibilities for the arguing, one of which was an argumentative style of communication between the parents. The mother sought me out after the talk to confide in me that, indeed, both she and her husband were lawyers, and that they frequently disagree openly in front of their children.

As a team, parents have the opportunity to model cooperation.

Summary Advice

- Treat children fairly, not necessarily equally.
- Don't make comparisons.
- Encourage individuality.
- Plan cooperative activities.
- Separation is often more effective than parent mediation.
- A parent team models cooperation.

Continual Conflict Between Brothers

I am writing for some advice and hints on how to handle the relationship between my two sons. Will just turned three and Nick is fourteen months old. The problem is that there is continual conflict between them. They do play well together. They also both play well alone when the other is gone, and get along well with the other children in their day-care groups. They don't display a lot of jealousy over attention from Mom and Dad.

It turns out that if I am to intervene only when one is hurting the other, as you suggest in your books, I must intervene every time they fight. I feel like I am intervening too much (and definitely more than I want to have to!), but don't know when not to, since there is always physical fighting involved. I'm also concerned about the effects on the children.

Although I usually suggest that parents' continued intervention may serve to increase the fighting and that siblings can work many arguments out by themselves, that recommended approach is more appropriate for school-age children who can verbalize their conflicts and can learn to compromise. For very young children, your interventions are appropriate. You can accomplish much by distracting toddlers, by bringing in different toys, and explaining simply about sharing. Separating the two children when they become too physical is effective for both preschoolers and school-age siblings. Ten minutes in separate rooms is usually enough for them to come peaceably together again, at least for a little while.

If you can manage some separate attention for Will when Nick is sleeping, it will help him to cope better with his younger brother's behaviors and reassure him that he doesn't have to share everything with him. Two brothers close in age are often very competitive, and, as they get older, you will definitely want to intervene less. You'll also find that as your children get busy with sports and games that these will become appropriate channels for their competition.

"Me First Always" Child

I have a "me first always" child. How do I convey to him that he doesn't always have to be the first one? He is four years old and his brother is two.

First, let me assure you that your son is not alone. There are many four-year-old "me firsters" out there and even more firstborns at that age who expect to be first in line. After all, he was there first—before his brother, that is.

I suggest you patiently explain to the boys in concrete terms that they need to take turns. Don't bother asking your son how he would feel if his brother always wanted to be first. He isn't at a cognitive stage of development where he can put himself in another person's place. If you insist the boys take turns being first and follow through consistently, your sons will both soon get the idea. If nothing else is accomplished, your younger boy will soon learn to assert himself to be sure he gets his turn at being first. You may have to ignore your older son's occasional crying, but consistency really pays off with teaching "turn taking."

Sisters Who Name Call

My daughters are two years apart in age and usually play well together. However, when they have a fight about anything, it usually results in their calling each other names. Most of the names are silly and harmless, as in "dork," or other "toilet" names, but they are either angry or hurt and complain to me that they've been called names. Sometimes I'm sure they have no idea of what the names even mean.

When preschool children argue and fight with one another, they tend to need some mediation by parents. Helping each to explain their point of view or their frustrations may permit you to teach them how to share, take turns, or compromise. The name calling is a shortcut for the expression of their anger, and at this age it is easier for them to use name calling than to talk it through. It is also a substitute for hitting each other, because they probably realize they would get into trouble if they were physical. It's best if you can help your daughters to talk through their differences, but if the name calling continues, it may be time for ten-minute separations.

14

Temper Tantrums

M ost children exhibit at least some temper tantrums during their preschool years. There are usually two main causes for tantrums: The first is frustration—blocks have fallen down, for example, or children don't have the words to express what they're feeling. The second is disappointment—children don't get what they want when they want it. Temper tantrums are often exacerbated when the child is hungry or tired, and as a matter of fact, hungry or tired is actually a third cause of temper tantrums.

The Frustration Tantrum

Learning to recognize the causes of tantrums helps parents to teach children more appropriate forms of temper control. For the frustration variety of tantrum, a parent may simply respond with a patient reminder to use words or a simple statement like "Come back to your blocks later." If parents have already tried those simple responses, ignoring the child or walking away may be appropriate.

The Disappointment Tantrum

For the disappointment tantrum, parents need to distract the toddler or preschooler, but remain firm. Giving in to children's inappropriate demands only leads to increased tantrums. This is not a time for negotiating. You may first want to walk away from a disappointment tantrum. Sometimes that's enough to quiet a child. However, if the tantrum is out of control, you'd do better to time your child out. Time-out on a chair, in a crib, or in the children's rooms are appropriate responses to the disappointment tantrums. If children fall asleep after the tantrum, there's a good chance that tiredness was a primary cause, or perhaps the tantrum itself was tiring.

Too Much Talk

As a general guideline, it's important for children to understand the problem, so simple explanations are always appropriate. Listening to children's points of view is also important. The system breaks down when parents spend too much time discussing or arguing with children. The continued discussion becomes an attention-getter and actually encourages more tantrums.

Team Response

Tantrums in children increase dramatically when adults disagree on how to respond to them. A team approach is a priority for tantrums. If Grandmom says yes after Mom or Dad have said no, or Dad gives in after Mom says no (or vice versa), the parent who appears to be the kind one is usually at fault and is, in effect, sabotaging the other parent. If Mother ignores the tantrum and Dad tries to comfort or hold the child, the tantrums will increase, particularly when both parents are around. Not only is this likely to encourage worse tantrums, but at least one parent will feel powerless in the process. If disagreement between adults happens regularly, you can expect temper tantrums to happen even more regularly. Your children are learning to manipulate adults because they don't know what to expect, or at least they have reason to expect they can get what they want, even though someone has told them no.

Summary Advice

- Identify the cause of the tantrum.
- Encourage the child to use words.
- Try to give simple explanations, which are important.
- Use the effective time-out if necessary.
- Avoid too much talk, which is counterproductive.
- Respond to tantrums as a team.

Tantrums Instead of Help

I have a four-year-old granddaughter who is sweet and precious until she is asked to do something, then she has a tantrum. What do you do to stop this, short of spanking?

Perhaps part of the problem is that you're asking your granddaughter instead of telling her. Sometimes children who are asked regularly assume they have a choice. If they choose not to do what they've been asked, parents and grandparents become frustrated and then insist.

If you want your granddaughter to take responsibility, tell her so. Also, if it's a new chore, she'll learn better if you work together on it and follow it with an activity. For example, cleanup time with Grandma could be explained this way: "Samantha, we'll pick up the toys together before our snack. You're a very good helper." In that way, Samantha feels valued, gets your attention, and learns to help. As she matures, she'll think of herself as a good helper and will become more skilled at the chore. She'll soon do it on her own by habit because she's learned the responsibility.

After all, picking up toys isn't really fun. Children wouldn't usually choose to do it if given a choice. Adults accomplish chores because they like the result—the neat house. Four-year-olds really aren't much interested in whether the house is neat. Incidentally, I'm glad you're not spanking.

15

Aggressiveness and Assertiveness

Biting, hitting, pushing, kicking, teasing, and bullying in a mean-spirited way are characterized as aggressive behaviors. Parents become concerned that their children may become "bullies" or just "mean" kids. Parents of children who are victims of aggressive behavior become anxious because their children are vulnerable and are fearful about their getting hurt. The second group of parents also worry that their children are not assertive enough.

Biting

Biting is an aggressive behavior that may not even be intended as aggressive. It is not at all uncommon for children between approximately eighteen months and three years of age to bite other children or adults. Sometimes it appears that the children who bite aren't even expressing anger or frustration but are being playful. The biting may even begin as a kiss. Other times, the biting seems to come out of frustration, almost like a tantrum. Many parents, especially the parents of victims, become upset about biting, and even preschool teachers sometimes overreact, as if "there is something very wrong with this child." Biting only represents a stage for children, and while not all children go through the stage, the problem always disappears, usually quite rapidly.

The first response to a child who bites you is a "No, no, you must not bite." An "ow" response will also help your child understand that he or she hurt you. If you say no in a different and raised voice, your child may never bite again, and you'll be done with the problem. Some toddlers don't heed that advice, however, even when given strongly. They try biting again. If the child is verbal, follow the "No, no" with "Use words." If your toddler isn't verbal yet, take her little hand and pat the place where she's bitten you and say, "Don't bite; make nice instead," or some other simple expression that feels comfortable to you. If biting follows again (and it may), follow steps one and two and add to that a brief time-out in the crib with an accompanying "No biting." Expect tears and maybe even a nap.

Preschool teachers can use a similar procedure. If cribs are not in use, a stern reprimand and a time-out chair away from the other children will convey the message. Although there may be several biting episodes before the problem is solved, they rarely exceed half a dozen. If it does become a continuous problem, it is worth seeing a psychologist to determine if there is a more serious problem underlying the biting. Only occasionally is that the case.

Some parents have tried the "biting back" approach and claim that it works. I won't recommend it because parents are modeling aggressive behavior, which is what they're trying to deter. Sometimes toddlers even think biting is a new game. I doubt if there is any "biting back" research, and I tend to think that when parents try it and it makes the biting worse, they keep the information to themselves. On the other hand, when it does work, they brag about it to others.

As for the parents of victims of biting behaviors, please don't threaten to sue the preschool or take your child out of the school. Be patient. Carefully nurse your child's wound, and explain that Freddy will soon stop. Your child and Freddy may turn out to be best friends someday after Freddy learns to use his mouth for talking instead of biting others.

Hitting, Pushing, and Teasing

Although hitting, pushing, shoving, kicking, and teasing can also be normal from time to time, a pattern of such aggressive behavior becomes high risk for physical bullying. These behaviors should be treated in a similar way to biting, except children may be more verbal, and explanations will be helpful. You can intervene and teach substitute behaviors to preschoolers with cue words like "share," "take turns," "be gentle," "use words," "Jesse is your friend," "say you're sorry." If the child repeats the aggressive hitting soon afterward, a time-out on a chair or in a room is appropriate. Try not to make comments like, "Why are you always so mean?" or "Why do you always start the fights?" Preschoolers can't answer those questions, and they start to feel as if they can't control the naughty behavior. Don't assume that your child is aggressive because they occasionally behave that way. All children do from time to time. You only need to teach them right from wrong, but it sometimes takes awhile. This is just another example of the importance of your being patient. However, don't ever just accept the aggressive behavior. It does require correction.

Causes of Aggressive Behavior

While it is true that some children are born with more aggressive temperaments than other children, environment does play an important part in either fostering or inhibiting bullying behaviors. There are many potential causes of aggressive behaviors.

Victims. Some children who are too aggressive have been the victims of aggressive behavior. Abusive parents, siblings, peers, or child-care providers can be imitated by the abused, and children who are "picked on" or abused by others surely do pick on other children. However, it is dangerous to assume that all aggressive children are being abused themselves. There are definitely other causes.

Overindulgence. Overindulgence can also cause children to act too aggressively. If children are accustomed to getting what they want when they want it, they may become verbally or physically aggressive with other children because they have been overempowered and do not believe in sharing or delaying their immediate wishes. They may even bully their parents and siblings.

Roughhousing. Aggressive behaviors may also be imitations of play for some children. Roughhousing and fun teasing may be defined as love for children, and hitting and touching become an automatic way of interacting. They may not understand they are being aggressive, but their activities are interpreted by others as aggression. If that seems to be an issue in your home, it's relatively simple for you to curtail the aggressive play. If it's family tradition, however, it may not be so easy to get Uncle Charlie to stop the fun wrestling. Incidentally, there's no need to stop it if your children aren't acting aggressively. They probably understand the difference.

Television and video games. Watching violence and aggressive behavior on television also fosters aggression in children. Sometimes children's programming involves as much aggressive behavior as adult videos. Even cartoons can model aggressive behavior. Video games are also often violent and inappropriate.

Parent sabotage. Another important source of aggressive behavior is parents who are not parenting as a team. If a parent takes the children's side against the other parent or other adult, aggressive and manipulative behavior is often the result because children are given more power than one of their parents. They are actually learning disrespect from a parent who is being disrespectful to the other parent (see chapter 9). This is especially challenging during or after divorce.

Anger. Aggressive behavior can result from inner anger children feel because something has gone wrong in their childhood that they don't understand. For example, adopted or foster children who may have been neglected in infancy or children who are being brought up in stressful environments that involve predivorce arguing, serious adult health problems, or other traumatic situations, could be acting out their unconscious unhappiness and frustrations.

Illness and allergy. Tension and frustration that result from illness, allergy, or deficits that parents may not be aware of can lead children to act out aggressively. Allergies to basic foods that children consume regularly, such as milk or wheat, could be culprits. Hearing, visual, or intellectual deficits that children can't explain to parents can cause frustration and lack of understanding that result in angry or aggressive behavior. It's important to check with your pediatrician or family doctor if you don't understand the reason for your child's aggressive behavior.

Prevention of Aggressive Behaviors

You can see by the long list of potential causes of aggressive behavior that parents may need to be detectives to determine potential causes. Removing violent role models, setting limits, team parenting, and teaching children to verbally express their anger are all helpful. Under no circumstances should you make excuses for aggressive children that can be interpreted by the children as condoning their behavior because of their problems. There should always be a consequence when children bully other children. For the most part, time-outs are effective, but sometimes you will need to make a stronger statement, such as taking away a party or a play date with a friend. Your serious disappointment in their behavior can be powerful in deterring them. A statement like "You must *never*, you hear me, absolutely *never* hit a child again!" will be a clear and appropriate message to an aggressive child.

Teach kindness and respect. Read stories to children about kindness and praise their kind behaviors. Be sure to point out and value the kind behaviors of other children and adults.

Taunted Children

If your children are victims of bullies, you'll need to help them know whether they should just walk away from aggressive children, whether being assertive will be appropriate, or whether they are in such danger that they must simply get the assistance of an adult. Crying seems to aggravate most problems, so you will have to teach your sensitive child to be more resilient and to try not to cry when just being teased and not being physically hurt. Holding back tears can be very difficult for some children.

The risk of overprotection. You will also want to listen to the child's feelings, while being careful not to be overprotective. The tears that flow after a child is taunted or teased are real. Even if the child has not been physically hurt, he may cry. It's not a good idea to encourage that oversensitivity even if feelings have been hurt. As he explains to you the name he's been called, you should explain that you understand that he feels hurt, but being called a bad name doesn't really have to hurt, and he can be strong. The old rhyme from your childhood "Sticks and stones will break my bones, but names will never hurt me" has been passed through many generations to arm the sensitive child against name callers.

If children receive too much attention when they are taunted, they sometimes unconsciously start a pattern of using any small taunt as an attention getter. The extra attention they receive may encourage them to get into the habit of playing the victim, and they may tattle and tease and put themselves in a position in which they are readily victimized. It becomes the only role they know how to play, and they may require help in learning how to play and be friends with other children. Give your children some tools to use in taking care of themselves, but don't make their victim status the center of family attention.

Here are some examples of the kinds of responses you can give to your children, depending on the extent of the physical or emotional battering they've received:

"Bonnie, you can just walk away from Joseph. You know he teases other kids as well."

"Rachel, remember that *you* are in charge. If you don't want Lenny to chase you at school, just stop, turn around, and look at him. He can't chase if you don't run away."

"Peter, just tell William to cut it out and that you won't play with him if he can't keep his hands to himself. If he quits, you can keep playing. If not, go play with Aaron or one of your other friends."

"Arielle, if you think you're really in danger of being hurt, go to the crossing guard or playground supervisor. If she doesn't help, ask if you can call me at work. But, Arielle, don't call unless you are really afraid you'll be hurt and you need an adult. You can usually handle a kid your own size, but if it's a big kid, that's when you may need the help."

Differentiating tattling and reporting. It is always difficult for children and even adults to determine when children should report taunting or physical abuse to adults. Even young children worry that they will be called tattletales, and parents become concerned that other children will tease and taunt further. Preschool teachers and parents alike should help children to understand the difference between tattling and reporting. Tattling involves telling an adult they require help when they can handle the situation themselves by either walking away or telling the other child to stop what he's doing. Tattling also involves telling an adult just to get the other child in trouble. Children should be encouraged not to tattle.

On the other hand, when children fear that they or someone else will be physically hurt, or if they see someone who has been physically hurt, they should report this to an adult. Preschool children may certainly require an adult to resolve a bullying situation. If a child is aware that someone has stolen something from another child, that, too, should be reported. Preschool teachers may wish to determine other rules for reporting; for example, if there are rules for bad language, the teacher may ask that children report such language. If children are not given specific behaviors to report, they are likely to be confused about whether to report them or not and may be afraid of being called that terrible epithet, "tattletale."

As parents, you can see that teaching sensitivity and kindness as you also teach assertiveness and resilience are not easy in a society that is itself confused about its values in this arena.

Summary Advice

- Teach substitute behaviors for biting, hitting, and kicking.
- Use a consequence for aggressiveness.
- Remove violent TV or video games.
- Demonstrate respect through team parenting.
- Teach and model kindness.
- Never condone bullying.
- Help children determine whether to walk away, be assertive, or get help.
- Avoid overprotection.
- Differentiate tattling from reporting.

Auntie Bites Back

While I was visiting my brother, his wife, and their children, their three-year-old son bit me. I took his arm and bit him back, but not hard enough to draw blood. Since then, he's never bitten again. His parents could not believe that neither one of them had thought of biting him back. The boy had no idea he was hurting anyone.

Questions about children who bite cross my desk frequently, and your answer, to bite back, has been recommended to me before. While I've tried chewing on that solution, I continue to find it indigestible.

No one likes children to bite them; it's truly painful. Although you may be correct in assuming your nephew doesn't know he is hurting someone when he bites, I can't ever recommend that an adult should model violent behavior or even that an adult should reduce him- or herself to a child's level of acting out. Instead, I suggest teaching the child replacement behavior by saying "no" very firmly and teaching the child to pat, kiss, or hug instead. That often works, but if it doesn't, a reprimand and a prompt time-out is almost always effective. Even if you hadn't bitten your nephew, he might never have bitten again. The biting stage hardly ever lasts very long, and at least children learn that adults don't bite.

Girl Doesn't Like "No"

I have a three-year-old daughter who doesn't like the word no. *She gets upset and hits and scratches people when she is angry. What can I do to get her to stop this?*

Most people, both big and small, do not like the word *no*. At some point, all of us have to learn to accept *no*es. Here are a few things that you can do that will help her reduce her anger and frustration.

First of all, it is important that your daughter learns that "no" means "no." This means that you and your child's other child-care providers need to give her a consistent message. When you have decided that she cannot have something, don't let her negotiate with you. Be firm.

Teach your child that hitting and scratching are not allowed by first explaining to her that it's wrong and giving her an opportunity to talk about her anger. If she repeats the hitting and scratching, put her in time-out by telling her to go to her room or a special place in the house for five minutes or until she calms down. Ignore her calling out to you. Then, when she has calmed down and the time is up, allow her to come out of the room and continue playing. You don't need to keep discussing the problem. After a few of these time-outs, she will learn not to hurt others when she's angry.

16

Fears

Fears are a natural part of preschoolers' lives, although some children experience more fears than others. Parents report a variety of children's fears at different stages of development. Many children are fearful of the dark, sleeping alone, thunderstorms, ghosts under the bed or in the closet, fires (especially during Fire Prevention Week), accidents that might happen to themselves or their family members, etc. These common fears take place when children are exposed to something in life that they don't understand or feel they can't control. Usually, a sympathetic explanation, a light left on, a door left open, and a comforting hug are sufficient to allay these fears. Although for some children these fears may be more persistent than for others, these are very normal fears that all children experience temporarily. You will want to help your children understand their fears, although too much talk may cause them to be more fearful.

Bad Dreams

Nightmares, or what children call "bad dreams," are the most annoying of all fears. They seem to emerge at different stages and rarely occur for only one night at a time. Initially, children need comfort, a drink of water, or a trip to the bathroom. A night-light and sometimes a full light can help them get back in the habit of sleeping through the night. It's not a good idea to comfort your children by having them join you in bed. While an occasional exception for thunderstorms will cause absolutely no problem, sleeping in a parent's bed can be a comfortable solution for children but an uncomfortable one for parents. If nightmares are becoming a regular pattern, be sure the child isn't watching TV within the hour and a half before bedtime. Research tells us that children don't sleep as well after watching TV. Stars or stickers on a calendar for sleep-through nights rapidly add up to better sleep for all. However, the fears are real, so they won't disappear immediately. Be patient and persevering as your children learn to be courageous.

Coping Tools

When children have fears, they have difficulty distracting themselves from thinking about their fears. A form of distraction that seems to help them feel like they can control their fears is to give them some tools to protect themselves. For example, for the child who is fearful of the dark, supply a flashlight that he can keep near him in his bed or if he goes upstairs alone. A small shelter in the basement equipped with special treats, books, or toys will make a child who is fearful of storms feel safe until the thunder passes. Sometimes a simple distraction like reading to a child during a thunderstorm is enough to help the child feel brave. Some parents teach children to say, "Go away, bad dreams" or use "magic words" to make fears go away. Words do help children feel brave.

Especially Fearful Children

Some children seem to be more fearful than others. They may require a little more preparation than others for new experiences. Knowing what to expect helps them to feel more confident. There are two precautions you may wish to be especially sensitive to for children who are particularly fearful. The first is related to referential speaking and the other to the choices that you give them.

Referential speaking. Referential speaking, as discussed earlier, is the adult talk children hear around them. If they're frequently referred to as shy or their fears are discussed by the adults around them, it becomes much more difficult for them to cope with their shyness and their fears. They assume they can't do anything about those problems. It's better not to talk at all about their shyness or fears within their hearing but to discuss them in terms of the new, more positive behavior you're seeing, as in, "Sonya seems to have gotten over most of her shyness" or "Alex is really quite brave." Even when other adults refer to your child as shy, you can politely contradict their observations by adding that "Sarah will warm up with just a little time and is much more social than she used to be." These positive statements are very effective in building confidence in your fearful children.

Choices. If you ask fearful children if they'd like to visit a new friend or take swimming lessons, they'll likely say no as a result of their fearfulness. This is likely to precipitate a power struggle in which you will attempt to allay their fears and convince them to invite the friend or take the lessons. You will probably give up and your children will become more fearful. Instead, assert positively that they may have a friend over or that they will begin swimming lessons and love them. They'll accept your expectations and adjust with your positive support. As they become more confident, you can give them more choices. You can also give them the choice of which friend they'd like to invite over or if they'd like to take swimming or gymnastics.

Preparation. Fearful children may also be more sensitive children. As you help them adjust to new risk-taking experiences like riding a bicycle, going to preschool for the first time, or going to a birthday party, you may wish to think about how you can break up each new experience into small steps. For example, before the birthday party you can describe to your children what they can expect. Your children can play birthday party with their dolls, and you can invite the child who is having the party to your home so your children get to know her better. Also, you may teach your children specific skills to use at a birthday party or on the bus or at preschool. You might teach them to introduce themselves to another child by saying, "Hi, my name is Jon. What do you like to play with on the playground?" or "What do you like to play with at preschool?" You could even role-play with your children so they can feel more comfortable. If you add a little silliness to the role-playing, they'll soon be laughing with you, and that, too, will remove some of the tension they may feel.

If you wish to validate your children's feelings of fear and also help them to adjust, you could say, "Sometimes I get a little afraid in a new situation, but the feeling goes away quickly because I soon start to like what I'm doing." Don't use statements such as, "I know how worried you are," or your children are likely to feel even more worried. Don't let your children sense that you are anxious about their adjustment. The calmer you act, the more easily they'll adjust. I used the term "act" intentionally. When your children are especially fearful, it's difficult for parents not to become overanxious, but you can put on a good act, and that, too, will be effective in fostering your children's courage.

Summary Advice

- Help children understand their fears.
- Avoid TV-watching before bedtime to prevent bad dreams.
- Stars or stickers may help build courage.
- Give children tools to help them cope with their fears.
- Don't talk about children's fears within their hearing.
- Don't give fearful children too many choices.
- Prepare fearful children for new experiences.
- Try not to show your own anxiety.

Referring to Shyness

How can you stop strangers from saying your children are shy when they talk to the children in stores? The children will not speak to them.

I'm glad that you're not calling your children shy, because that's a common mistake that parents make about children. The term I use when adults talk to each other about a child as if the child isn't present is "referential speaking." Referential speaking is very powerful because children assume that if adults are saying something to each other, it's surely true. They often accept it as a label and may even assume that they can't change.

When other people comment about your children's shyness, you could point out to these people that they seem to be outgrowing their shyness, or that they're actually quite friendly and only need a little time to get to know you. If they hear these positive comments about themselves, they'll soon become friendlier and strangers will change their referential speaking.

Extremely Shy Girl

How can we help our tremendously shy three-and-a-half-year-old daughter?

Shy behaviors can be partly inherited and partly learned. Even biologically shy children can learn appropriate social involvement and usually do if parents don't overprotect or shelter them too much. However, don't insist on so much involvement that your daughter feels constantly pushed. Too much pressure could cause her to retreat further. If you can avoid either sheltering too much or pushing too much (both extremes), your daughter will learn to participate in a variety of activities, and will become more comfortable in most social environments.

Avoid power struggles. Don't get into a pattern of saying she should become involved and then permit her to persuade you to change your decision. Instead, assume she'll participate and stay positive.

You can use referential speaking as a positive technique for your shy daughter. Referential speaking is conversation between adults about children within the hearing of those children. It has potential for significant positive or negative impact on children, although more often than not it is used negatively for shy children. Adults often talk to each other about how shy these children are, and the children often accept shyness as a label and assume that they can't change. They believe that what the adults are saying about them to each other is always true.

Here's how you can use referential speaking to help your daughter: Say to your spouse when your three-and-a-half-year-old is within hearing, "Did you notice how friendly Rachel is becoming? She doesn't seem to be as shy as she used to be." You could also say to other people (grandparents, friends, and relatives) such statements as, "Have you noticed? Rachel seems to be outgrowing her shyness." This will reinforce her social behavior and help her change her self-image. You will find that positive referential speaking is remarkably effective in helping your daughter develop social confidence.

Boy Fears Noises

My two-year-old has developed a fear of noises. We live near an airport, and he is afraid to go out alone because of planes overhead. He gets upset and clings to me. I try to reassure him, but will this pass?

Although some children remain especially sensitive to sound, many two-year-olds respond to loud noises with extreme fear. As you describe your son, I recall my own two-year-old son clinging desperately to me, crying and saying, "I'm afraid of the funder."

For the most part, two-year-olds don't do much playing alone outside, so you can probably help him feel safe by going out with him for a little while each day until he gradually becomes accustomed to those low-flying planes. You may want to hold him and point to planes when they're farther away and not quite so noisy. Mainly, time is on your side. Most two-year-olds outgrow their fear of noises rather quickly.

Boy Fears Swimming Lessons

Our four-and-a-half-year-old was very excited when we enrolled him in swimming lessons. Now, after the first class, he cries and refuses to go. How do we handle this?

Swimming, or at least understanding simple water safety, becomes more important if you live near the water, have a swimming pool, or are planning a summer vacation near a lake or ocean. Although preschool children rarely become proficient swimmers, maintaining a healthy fear of dangerous water combined with an early introduction to playing in the water may be important for saving your son's life in a waterfront environment. It's worth explaining to your son that swimming lessons are critical for his safety.

Swimming instructors are usually well trained to gradually accustom small children to the water. Talk to the teacher and explain your son's fear. She'll probably let him sit on the side of the pool and dangle his feet at first. She may splash him gently or let him watch the other children. If she allows you to sit with him through one or two lessons, that may be helpful. If she prefers you don't, leave him confidently, and reassure him he'll be fine.

Children are often afraid to put their faces in the water. You might want to help him with this fear within the safety of the bathtub. Within a few weeks he'll be splashing around and smiling at you.

Unusual Separation Anxiety

My four-year-old has been refusing to stay at other people's houses to play with friends without me. She used to. She wants to have her friends at our house all the time. I have already tried not inviting kids until she goes to someone else's house, but it hasn't made her decide to go. This started in late summer but has gotten worse since preschool began.

Your daughter's new separation anxiety could stem from any one of a number of experiences. It could be something she saw on TV, or she could have heard an adult conversation that made her fearful that you wouldn't return, or perhaps you stayed away longer than you expected when she visited a friend, or, even more likely, something happened when she visited a friend that scared her. If she was actually frightened at a friend's home, it could be something innocuous like a mother scolding or correcting her or her friend. Of course, it could also be something more serious, like abuse, but I hope you know the friend's parents well enough to be reassured that no serious harm was done. I'm assuming that you've already asked your daughter if she is afraid of anything in particular, and her answers have not provided clues.

I would suggest reducing the number of times she can have friends at your home but not eliminating visits entirely. Explain that it is just too hard for you to constantly host friends, and it will be fine for her to play alone some of the time. Try not to turn the situation into a battle, and try to prevent your daughter from realizing that you're worried about her anxiety. Her sensing your anxiety would likely increase her anxiety.

Try to arrange occasional visits to her friends' houses where you can socialize with the friend's mother. Your presence will reassure her as she gradually gets in the habit of playing elsewhere. After a few such comfortable visits, find a reason for leaving briefly to permit her to adjust to your absence. By that time, she may feel comfortable again.

If your daughter's anxiety continues, or if she continues to be fearful about going to other homes even when you are there, you may require more detective work than I can give you in my column. A good psychologist can help you to determine if there are deeper issues involved in your daughter's anxieties.

Fear of Everything

My two-year-old daughter says she's afraid of everything. To be more specific, she's afraid of boys and men she doesn't know, hair in the bathtub, ceiling fans, balloons, reflections on the roof of the car at night, feathers, dirt on her hands, and the list goes on. I would call her fears excessive and quirky, and I'd like to know what's underlying them and what I can do to eliminate them.

Your daughter seems to be displaying more fears than are typical for even a two-year-old. However, two-year-olds have heightened awareness and sensitivity, and it isn't unusual for them to be either fearful or fascinated by ceiling fans or reflections.

Simple explanations may allay your daughter's fears. You can also ignore some that you've already explained several times. It's most important for you not to be overanxious about your child's anxiety. Most of these fears should disappear or come and go during the next year. If they continue or grow worse, be sure to check with a psychologist or psychiatrist for further help.

17

Food and Fitness

Although eating is natural, parents have the responsibility for encouraging children to eat a balanced diet. What seems to cause the unnecessary power struggles for many parents is children's frequent rejections of adult-style foods, their often narrow range of food preferences, and the variability of their hunger. Sometimes they seem to consume adultlike portions, and other times it seems they'd rather not eat at all. To help cope with parental anxieties about their children's eating, pediatricians usually suggest they view a balanced diet as that which children eat during the full week rather than for any one day. Some pediatricians even suggest observing your children's consumption over a period of a month to determine if they're getting good nutrition. Also, children's regular checkups with their pediatrician that show normal growth and healthy weight gain should be reassuring.

Do be patient about your children's eating. Although you do want your children to be healthy and develop appropriate nutritional habits, there is a reason that most restaurants provide children's menus that look a lot alike. There must be something consistent about children's tastes that is different from the diet that most adults prefer. Following are some tips to encourage preschoolers to eat well:

Tips for Healthy Preschool Eating

- If preschoolers tend to fill up on juices, water them down to provide fluids that aren't filling.
- Unsweetened cereals that can be eaten with the fingers make healthy snacks, and aren't as messy as some other cereals.
- To encourage children to eat crusts of bread, be sure to spread butter or peanut butter on them. To encourage them to eat the end piece of bread, face so the crust isn't visible.
- Plastic cups with lockable lids make drinks portable.
- Separate lunch bags for each child provide interest and independence.
- Try introducing new food when your child is hungry, but not starving or overtired. If time allows, the beginning of the breakfast or lunch meals may be the most conducive times. If weekdays are busy, try on the weekends, when everyone is more relaxed and you can sit with your child and have a more pleasant mealtime. Offer new foods at the beginning of the meal.
- Have kids sit at the table when eating a meal or snacks; they are more likely to think about whether they are hungry or full and are also less likely to be "grazers" who constantly have little snacks but eat poorly at meals. (By sitting at the table, your house will be cleaner and you will also decrease the likelihood of choking, which can happen more easily if children walk, run, or fall while they are eating.)
- Eliminate distractions at the table: no toys or TV.
- If kids resist eating vegetables, temporarily avoid the cooked variety, and let them start the meal with raw vegetables like baby carrots, celery, cucumbers, yellow squash circles, sugar snap peas, broccoli "trees," or small leaves of lettuce or cabbage. If they resist this, give them the option of dipping vegetables in a little bit of salad dressing that you put on their plate (that way, parents control the amount). Many kids will also try vegetables if they are in small bits and put on a pizza or mixed in with pasta.

- Alternative ways to get kids to eat dairy products are to add an ice cube to milk (some children dislike warm milk); "cool down" hot chocolate by adding more milk; make pudding with milk; buy frozen yogurt or yogurt in small cups (let the child choose if possible), and consider trying different fruit mixtures; serve any type of cheese, either cold or melted on bread, and cottage or ricotta cheese, either plain or topped with a small amount of fruit, granola, wheat germ, or chopped nuts.

- Alternative ideas for fruit: Let children choose some of the fruit in the grocery store; try some of the available "exotic" fruits like mangoes, kiwi, baby bananas, papaya, fresh pineapple, or melon varieties; let children help make a fruit salad of any combination of fruits; try sample size cans of new mixtures of cut fruit; serve dried fruit (there are many combinations available just about anywhere); make a fruit shake, mixing fresh or frozen fruit with yogurt and an ice cube in a blender; try putting frozen fruit in a small cup, cover it with milk, and let it sit a minute. This frozen fruit slush begs to be eaten with a spoon and is popular any time of the day.

- Consider alternative forms of protein: nuts; cheese cubes; hummus, either spread on bread or used as a dip with veggies; various lunch meats; tuna; eggs; turkey sausages; cottage or ricotta cheese; dried turkey "jerky"; baked beans or any other type of beans.

- All kids like sweets, so parents are frequently on the lookout for healthier options. Potential alternatives to standard sweets may include dry, sweetened cereal (may be sweeter than you want them to eat for breakfast but still a healthier sweet snack than the usual cookies, etc.); cereal bars; flavored mini rice cakes; graham crackers; pudding made with milk; dried fruit; frozen juice or yogurt; frozen yogurt.

- Allow children to help in the kitchen. All kids like to stir, add ingredients, watch a mixer work, sprinkle the cheese on the pizza, crack an egg, or use a whisk or a nut chopper. You don't have to allow it every day, but it can be a fun activity when time allows. Active participation in the project usually increases their interest in trying the finished project.

- To encourage healthy snacking (and independence), consider keeping one shelf or drawer in the refrigerator filled with easily accessible snack foods that children can get independently, such as string cheese, kid-size yogurt, juice, dried fruit, cut veggies, mini bagels, mini muffins. If space allows, plan a similar shelf in a cupboard. This clearly identifies what snacks are available to children and to any baby-sitter or grandparent who may be taking on snack duty.

- For travel, to store in your glove compartment or to keep on hand, try making your own trail mix of foods you want your children to eat. Possibilities include mixing any combination of the following from your cupboard: pretzels, raisins or other dried fruits, cheese crackers, squares of graham crackers, and dry cereal.

- If your child is a particularly picky eater, try having other kids offer encouragement to try foods. Food is always more appealing if another child has it.

- To prevent choking in young children, establish good eating rules. Only eat sitting down; never carry food around; only eat with an adult present in the room; and cut all food into small, noncircular bites. The most common choking items include uncut grapes, circular bites of hot dogs (cut them in half lengthwise as well as into slices); hard candy; small game pieces; deflated balloons; peanut butter (eliminate this problem by putting peanut butter between slices of bread and never leave uncovered).

- You can also make food issues and shopping more fun by letting your children pick out some items to put in the cart. Before doing this, make sure your child is aware of choices, and keep them simple: Do you want oranges or grapes? Pita bread or wheat bread? American cheese or Cheddar? If you want to have some control while giving children choices, clip coupons of items you approve of, and let your children use these to make selections (many coupons have pictures of the products, so kids love this game and become very proud of their selections). It is especially good with cereal and kid-size yogurt and can provide an easy way to avoid an argument as well: "We don't have a coupon for double-grape chocolate-covered sugar bomb cereal. You can choose any of the cereals on these coupons."

Courtesy of Janet Rimm

Picky Eaters

Offering very small portions of food at each meal encourages children to ask for more rather than rejecting food and becoming negative about mealtime. It's also less wasteful. Treats and snacks should be kept to a minimum and should follow a healthy meal, although exceptions can be made for holidays and surprises. If your children's only favorite food is peanut butter and jelly, you can limit it to once a day.

Adult role models for appropriate eating make a difference; for example, picky adults encourage picky children. You will want to mention aloud that you're enjoying new food, and you certainly want to be wary about negatively criticizing your spouse's or Grandma's cooking. Your children are listening to all your comments about food. It's also important that your children see you sit down at the table for a meal rather than constantly snacking. Parents who won't try new foods or eat only fast foods can expect children to copy these problematic patterns.

At a family holiday celebration, if you're the host, you can plan to include at least one food your picky eater enjoys. That may prevent a brouhaha, and maybe he'll also try a new food. It's not worth the turmoil to insist on new foods at a family celebration. Nutritional balance probably won't work out during the holidays, either, and you're better off letting the children know that the holidays are exceptions rather than disturbing the peace and fun at the time.

If Grandma or Grandpa provides a treat you'd prefer the children not to have, make the exception at the time, but do communicate your preference for the future. If you argue, you'll probably lose in the eyes of your parents (or in-laws) and your children both.

Allergies

Some children have food allergies, which means that parents will need to inform their children's preschools, the hosts where children visit for play dates or parties, and all child-care providers about those allergies. It's better to write a note about specific allergies and give it to anyone who is likely to be providing your children with food. The written information not only serves as a reminder to all other appropriate adults, but it prevents a lot of attention-getting discussion. It's helpful if you can be as matter-of-fact as possible so your allergic children don't begin thinking they are strange or unusual because of the allergy.

Overweight Children

Some children are overweight and eat too much. This can be a serious problem because lifelong eating patterns begin early, and obesity increases the risk of many illnesses. It is difficult to explain to preschool children that they've had enough when they are still hungry and wish to eat more. It's probably easier to provide nutritious and nonfattening foods for your overweight preschooler than limiting the quantity when they're hungry. Also remember to offer small servings. Children simply don't need as much food as adults.

Ask your doctor to recommend a child nutritionist to help you arrange a special diet for your overweight child. Be particularly sensitive about talking too much about weight loss, whether for your overweight child or yourself. If children hear too much about dieting and weight loss, they become anxious about their own weight. Try to tone down issues about your own weight problems or your spouse's (if either of you have them) and emphasize healthy eating habits rather than diets.

Staying United at Mealtimes

Serious eating problems often result when parents, or parents and grandparents, disagree openly and continually about children's eating. When one parent believes in the "clean plate club" and the other believes that children should eat what they choose, you can count on producing a picky or rebellious eater. Either approach will probably work if everyone agrees. If children are required by both parents to eat everything they're served, they probably will, provided they're given small servings and some exceptions are made. On the other hand, the concept of some choices at some meals fits with the way adults often prefer to eat, so if the choices are reasonable, that may also be acceptable. For example, choices are often given between cereals or breads at breakfast. Children could also choose a juice. At lunch children could select from one or two different types of sandwiches. At the evening meal, which often takes more preparation, there is usually one main course, and children should be expected to eat that so a parent doesn't have to cook something different for every member of the family.

You can see that there are a variety of correct approaches to planning meals for children. Parents can agree to make reasonable compromises about children's eating, or one parent can just go along with the approach the other parent has selected as long as an argument about it doesn't take place at mealtime. The team approach at mealtime is very important. Conflict can become one of the causes of later eating disorders, which can cause serious health problems.

Physical Fitness

It's important to get all children, and especially overweight ones, into good physical fitness habits early. Although most preschool children enjoy plenty of physical activity spontaneously, awkward or overweight children may be less attracted to physical activities without your insistence. Playgrounds give children opportunities to explore swinging, climbing, and balancing. Lessons such as gymnastics, tumbling, simple sports, and dance are important even if children's coordination is not particularly good. You will need to be particularly cafeful not to tease or ridicule children if they are awkward, or they'll soon shun the related activities. Incidentally, awkward children who become involved in fitness activities early often show great improvements in their coordination when given the opportunity to learn skills. Practice really does help, and during these early years, children are particularly sensitive to learning experiences in the physical as well as intellectual domain. With regular involvement in fitness experiences, their awkwardness often diminishes or even disappears. The example below describes a personal and inspiring story of Sara (I hope she will forgive me for sharing). Joining children in fitness experiences encourages them and provides good exercise for their parents as well.

How Fitness Can Improve Coordination

Our youngest daughter, Sara, had poor large muscle coordination as a preschooler. She didn't walk until she was twenty-one months old (I think that is some kind of record). I was told not to worry, but I did. She fell a lot and did seem somewhat awkward.

By age three, Sara was in gymnastics, dance, and swimming lessons. Fortunately, no one commented on her awkwardness as she learned to skip, hop, jump, and tumble. Sometimes there were comments about immaturity as a mask for commentary on her awkwardness, but the comments never prevented her regular lessons or her fun. Her lessons continued into her school years. Her dancing became quite graceful, and her tumbling fairly good. Swimming took extra perseverance. She repeated Advanced Beginners swimming classes eight times before she finally passed her test. I watched each trial and wondered if she'd ever pass. With each failure I gave her encouragement I didn't feel.

The perseverance was worthwhile. As a young adult, Sara is fit and above average in her physical coordination. She's a swimmer, certified lifeguard, biker, windsurfer, dancer (for fun), and shows absolutely no indication of the awkwardness that was hers as a preschooler. She recalls some of the awkwardness, but she was never deterred by it.

Summary Advice

- Consider a week's worth—rather than a day's—of eating for balanced nutrition.
- Provide small servings.
- Be role models of healthy eaters.
- Snacks and desserts follow meals.
- Adults should stay united at mealtime.
- Exercise regularly for fitness.

Negotiating with Hungry Children

What is your suggested strategy regarding eating/snacking/ sweets/ meal rules with two-and-a-half- and four-year-old children? We can't seem to avoid constant negotiation and/or hungry children.

Eating is a natural process, but preschoolers hardly ever eat in the way that parents expect or would like. A few children eat everything they're served, but most eat little food sometimes and much more at other times. Still other children drink quantities of milk and eat relatively little. Pediatricians tell us to look at children's nutritional consumption on a weekly basis rather than on a daily basis in order to determine if they're maintaining a balanced diet.

If you're trying to break your children of the habit of continuous "grazing," plan three meals and three snacks each day with a healthy snack halfway between meals and one more before bedtime. Serve very small helpings at each meal so your children are more likely to finish what you give them. They may even learn to ask for more.

Preschoolers can learn to ask to be excused from the table and clear their place after they've completed a meal. This will give them an understanding of routine by learning that each meal and snack has a beginning and an end, and it will prevent them from assuming that eating is continuous. Keep inappropriate snack food out of the house or save special treats for weekends or celebrations.

The combination of all these suggestions will diminish the battles and keep eating the pleasant and naturally healthy activity it's supposed to be.

Too Many Unhealthy Foods

My five-year-old son eats more than enough food and is growing beautifully; however, he chooses a very limited menu of mainly unhealthy foods. Peanut butter sandwiches are his mainstay. He'll also eat hot dogs, sugared cereal, crackers and cookies, chicken nuggets, and French fries. His vegetable is limited to cucumbers and his one fruit choice is apples. He does enjoy quantities of milk and apple juice. Although there may be a few foods I missed, I think you have the idea. I know his diet is far from balanced, but I hate to get into continued power struggles about food, and I know there are many children who tend to be limited in their tastes. Should I wait for him to grow up to expand his menu, or should I insist on his trying some other foods?

It doesn't take a nutritionist to know your son is eating too many fats and sweets and not enough fruits and vegetables. He'll surely grow, but he may also become overweight and have clogged arteries. Although I certainly do oppose power struggles about food, a little positive teaching could expand your son's menu and provide better balance.

Explain to your son the importance of a healthy diet, emphasizing that you'd like him to try new foods at least once a day. Add a very small serving of a vegetable or fruit or new protein (such as chicken, tuna, or cheese) to his regular peanut butter sandwich. Before he has a second sandwich, tell him you'd like him to keep trying these healthy new foods. A bite or two is all you need to insist on. Be sure to model eating these foods yourself until your son becomes accustomed to the new tastes. You could say, "I haven't eaten asparagus in years, but I'll try it again now that I'm older. My tastes have really changed, and I bet I'll like it now."

If your son refuses to try the new foods, explain that he can't have a second sandwich or dessert. He'll soon get the idea that trying new foods is a required part of healthy eating, and he'll undoubtedly expand the number of foods he'll eat gradually. He will soon begin to understand that healthy eating is important and will actually learn a little more about a balanced diet.

18

Sleep Issues

Children vary considerably in the amount of sleep they require, but the timing of bedtime, waking, and napping should be guided by parents. By the time a baby is three months old, a rhythm for sleep is often established, although for some babies it takes as long as a year. Furthermore, if parents don't establish routines that fit in with the household routines, bedtime may be a haphazard battle of wills instead of a pleasant independent ceremony. Reasonably regular naps and bedtimes lead to reasonably regular waking times. Pushing bedtime limits leads to difficulty in arousing a child in the morning.

Parents should design a bedtime that leaves some private time for themselves and that fits with a morning waking schedule. Pleasant routines, such as bath, snack, story time (read or told), conversations, quiet music or games, snuggles, and prayers are all appropriate ways to end a child's day happily and independently.

See the hints for pleasant bedtime routines at the end of this chapter.

Bedtime Avoidance

Many children are extraordinarily talented in avoiding bedtime. Somehow that talent disappears by parenthood, and you're left finding yourselves more tired than your children each evening. If your children's talent at avoiding bedtime exceeds your ability to stay awake, you'll find yourselves without any private adult time. This delayed bedtime produces tired children during the day and frustrated and discontented partners in marriage. Reasonable and consistent bedtimes produce happier adults and more alert, intelligent children.

Sometimes very young children manipulate parents into rocking them or carrying them around until they fall asleep. That used to be called "spoiling" a child, and it *still* is spoiling the child. Of course, there's nothing wrong with comforting or holding a child when he or she isn't well. All children should have plenty of hugs and cuddling. However, they should learn to fall asleep on a regular basis independently. This means that you may have to permit your children to cry themselves to sleep once or twice, which is usually all it takes. It's harder on you than it is on your children.

A baby who cries once in a while at bedtime probably requires comforting. If he or she cries regularly, you probably need the comforting. Give yourself permission to let your baby cry him or herself to sleep. If you're hesitant about letting your children cry too long, go to their room every fifteen minutes at first and pat them without taking them out of the crib or bed. Then extend the time between visits by five minutes each time until they finally fall asleep on their own. You may find yourself more comfortable with this approach. Both approaches work, but parents are often hesitant about using the cold-turkey approach.

Roughhousing, television, overstimulation, manipulation of bedtime, and an adult sleeping with a child are some of the inappropriate ways that prevent independent and calm rest.

Pacifying Devices

Pacifying devices including silky or soft blankets, favorite stuffed animals, dolls, bottles, pacifiers, and even thumb sucking provide an array of assists to help children sleep without depending on a parent to lie in bed with them. The first three devices often remain in use during the entire preschool period, and some six- and seven-year-olds continue to enjoy tucking their soft friends in with them. This doesn't seem to cause anyone any problems, except if they're forgotten on a visit, and children seem to give these up naturally, without much trauma.

Early thumb sucking doesn't cause any problems for children except in the minds of their parents, and the thumb conveniently is always available. Most children give up their thumbs quite naturally as well. For some children, however, sucking thumbs continues beyond bedtime, and dentists caution that it may cause dental problems. It doesn't seem sensible to encourage thumb sucking to pacify your child. A pacifier seems to be a better approach. You can reserve it for naps and sleep and take it away when toddlers outgrow its need, without worrying about its adverse effect on teeth or developing verbal skills.

Bottles are also effective for pacifying, but dentists caution against milk residue on children's new teeth. Of course, breast-fed babies also get milk residue, yet no one seems worried about mother's milk. Although water seems to do no harm, it is less appealing to babies than milk. If this seems to be a little confusing to you as parents, the confusion gives you choices, none of which are perfect, but also none of which cause babies major problems.

Some parents in desperate efforts to get enough sleep have put television sets on in children's rooms to keep them quiet. While that may be a good short-term solution, it's likely to cause long-term problems. The television will likely keep children's attention and prevent them from disturbing parents, but it will prevent getting into good sleeping habits. Quiet music is a better solution for children who have difficulty falling asleep. Lullabies have always been useful for "lulling" children into dreamland. They don't have the adverse effect of turning small children into night people who become glued to a television screen and dependent on visual stimulation.

Bedtime Fears

Don't let bedtime fears become an avoidance technique. If children are afraid or worried about ghosts, permit them to leave on a hall light or night-light or provide a flashlight, as suggested in chapter 16. Finding a way for children to handle their fears without becoming dependent on a parent is important. That means that you don't go to sleep with them at night or tuck them into your bed or permit them to sleep on the living room sofa. Of course, the occasional exception is always acceptable.

One plan for handling children's fears that often works well is to permit two siblings to sleep in the same room. Fearful children even feel comforted when they can share their room with their baby brother or sister. Sometimes children enjoy sleeping with a pet. This is obviously a matter of personal preference because some parents would never consider it, and sleeping with pets is definitely not appropriate for babies or toddlers. Eventually, all children should be able to sleep alone as part of the encouragement of their independence. In homes where there simply isn't enough room to give children a room of their own, having one child go to bed before the other gives a child the opportunity to be in a room alone and learn to be brave.

Postponing Bedtime

When both parents have busy careers, they become tempted to let their children stay up late at night so they can have more quality time with them. They often feel guilty about the time spent away from their preschoolers and are vulnerable to children pushing their bedtime limits. If children stay up late, they may be hard to wake in the morning for day care or preschool, which can cause either insufficient sleep for your preschooler and/or continuous power struggles about rising and dressing in the morning. These are bad habits to start because they become difficult to adjust when children attend school.

Keeping children up late limits adult private and quiet time. For either a married couple or a single adult, quiet time before bedtime is important. Consider that half of marriages end in divorce, and divorce always causes trauma for children. If you're considering what's best for your children, adult time devoted to preserving

Making Bedtime Pleasant

- Bedtime becomes less stressful for everyone if a night routine is set up for children. Our children used to call it their "ceremonies." That framework permits children to expect bedtime and avoids their making it into a nightly exercise in avoidance. If there's a reasonably regular structure, children actually respond more flexibly to exceptions.

- To establish a bedtime routine, make a list with your children of pre-bedtime tasks. The list might include bath, dress in pajamas, take clothes out for the next day, brush teeth, etc. Have them tape the list to their mirror or wall. You can make little pictures to help preschoolers remember the order of tasks. The final activities of the list might be having a snack, a parent reading, chatting time, and quietly looking at books in bed. Some activities may vary with family preferences.

- Now ask your children to follow their list and be sure that you don't nag them through it. The final activities, snacks, story time, etc., are dependent on whether the first are accomplished on time. When you explain this to your children, be positive. Don't threaten. Just say, "Hurry and do all the things on the list so we can have more time for reading tonight."

- Once children have completed their "ceremonies," explain that they *must* stay in their own rooms. If they insist on calling to you every few minutes or coming out to interrupt you, warn them once that if it continues, you'll have to close and latch their door until they fall asleep. Assure them that you'll open it once they're asleep. Usually the warning is enough for them to know that you're serious, but for some children, you may want to use that latch once or twice. If they're frightened, leave a light on. Your intention is not to punish, but to set a definite limit.

- If your children cry after you've closed the door, after fifteen minutes open the door and explain that if they're ready to sleep quietly, you will open it again.

- Be sure to make exceptions for special occasions or weekends. Children respect fair rules better than rigid ones. However, do enforce the bedtime rules regularly for their sake and your own.

a marriage is a reasonable investment for all of you. If you are a single parent, adult time preserves a place to put things in perspective and makes it less likely you will become dependent on your children for company. Although you should certainly enjoy and love your children, it is not fair to depend on them for emotional sustenance.

United Sleep Routines

All adults who live with children (parents, friends, grandparents) need to be consistent with one another about bedtime guidelines, or bedtime will surely become a battleground. Exceptions on the weekend can provide some flexibility, but for preschoolers, even these exceptions can be fraught with crankiness. Sleep is another area in which parents must work as a team to prevent stressful bedtimes.

Summary Advice

- Establish positive routines.
- Avoid overstimulation.
- Consider pacifiers, music, stuffed animals, or siblings for help.
- Encourage independence.
- Don't postpone bedtime.
- Keep a team approach.

Can Reducing Pacifier Use Cause Nightmares?

I have a question about my four-and-a-half-year-old son. He is a wonderful kid, very inquisitive, has a great sense of humor, and except for being a bit shy around adults whom he doesn't know particularly well, is very social and has a number of friends. But, he still relies quite heavily on his pacifier, and although my wife and I have worked successfully to limit its use, he stills uses it when going to bed, and in other situations when he is upset and/or tired. He has definitely reduced its use.

Now, in the last week or ten days, my son has awakened at night (fairly early in his sleep) with what are either nightmares or night terrors. He doesn't seem to truly "snap out of it," and envisions monsters or shadows in his room. Fortunately, they are short-lived; last night it lasted for only minutes and he went back to bed right away and slept straight through the night. Typically, he is a good sleeper, although he has gone through some rough periods. These seem, at least most recently, to be related to my wife not lying in bed with him to help him get to sleep.

I wonder if these recent night terrors are directly related to our withdrawing the pacifier. It has, unfortunately, been an all too important emotional stabilizer for him. In fact, even in the car the other day, he wanted it, and we hadn't brought it with us, and he "flipped out," crying and even saying he was very scared. He did finally calm down, and we had a wonderful time for the rest of the day. Does this seem plausible—the connection between our attempt to wean him from his use of the pacifier and the development of these night terrors? What might we do to ease his transition away from the pacifier?

Nightmares are common for children between the ages of about three and six and sometimes even beyond. Although it's impossible to determine if they're related to your son's pacifier withdrawal or to your wife's distancing herself at night, they could just as easily be related to a scary picture he may have seen on TV, which may be completely unrelated to his real life.

At age four-plus, your son is far beyond the need for a pacifier, and you may be more anxious about discontinuing its use than he will be once the task is accomplished. Explain to your son that he's growing up, and children his age don't usually use pacifiers. Tell him that you're planning to throw it away and give him a new stuffed animal to sleep with instead. Then follow through, and be sure you no longer have a pacifier in the house.

Your son may cry the first night. Reassure him once or twice that he is a big boy and you love him very much and are sure he'll be all right without his pacifier. You might even want to add a little quiet music to soothe him. Then be firm. He'll soon be fast asleep, and by the third night, he'll not even ask for his pacifier. The "bad dreams" may continue for a while, and although annoying, will probably disappear after a few nights.

Bedtime Problems

We have developed a problem when putting our child to bed. We are working parents of a three-and-a-half-year-old, and our schedules are routine—leave by seven-thirty and return home by five-thirty or six. We felt early on that we missed our child and wanted to keep him up so we could spend time with him each night reading and having a snack before bedtime. However, we also laid down with him until he fell asleep. We are now having a problem in breaking this habit. Do you have any suggestions?

Infants are flexible enough to learn their parents' preferred routines, and your three-and-a-half-year-old son has learned them well. Actually, your loving time together, reading and sharing a snack, are typical of appropriate routines many parents follow in order to spend time with their children at the end of their workday. It's the lying down with your son until he falls asleep that has enslaved you. You've accidentally taught your little boy to be dependent on you for going to sleep. You're not alone. Far too many parents find themselves tied to their children's bed, and some even take their children into their own bed.

Dependence that is fostered by sleeping with parents on a regular basis is not healthy for children's emotional growth and has other negative implications for the parents' adult relationships. I don't think I have to convince you because you already recognize it as a problem, but many parents continue to sleep with their children assuming it will make them feel more secure. The longer children depend on a parent in their bed, the more traumatic the breaking away will be. Fortunately, your son is only three-and-a-half. The habit should be fairly easy to change.

Explain to your son that he is now old enough to sleep on his own. Expect to see a few tears; he'll probably cry or complain. Suggest that he hug some stuffed animals, and explain that you'll be happy to leave a small light on in his room if he'd like. Emphasize that neither of you will sleep with him anymore. Assure him you'll leave his door open if he can fall asleep quietly, but will close it if he continues to cry or scream. Remind him that you'll open the door when he's quiet. Then give him a good-night hug and a smile that masks the anxiety you feel, and leave the room.

If your son gets out of bed and follows you, take him back to bed and close the door. Fisher-Price makes a plastic safety doorknob that prevents a child from being able to open the door. Be prepared. Your son may cry and scream the first time. Don't respond. He will finally fall asleep, although you may find him on the floor near the door.

When all is quiet, be sure to open the door. As you arrange the covers around your sleeping angel, you'll have the satisfaction of knowing you've taught him to take an important difficult step toward independence. By the second night, he'll go to sleep with no more than a whimper, and although he may complain for a few days about the difficulty of falling asleep on his own, he will soon learn to enjoy sleeping alone, and you may again be able to enjoy your much deserved adult time together at the end of a hardworking day.

Many children push bedtime limits. They seem energetic, tireless, and eager to be little adults. They often want to stay with their parents until their parents go to sleep. While all this seems natural, parents who yield to their children's pressure find themselves feeling overwhelmed and cheated. Once bedtime rituals are firmly established, they can become pleasant ends to the day. Be sure to make exceptions to the routines for special occasions, but if there are no routines, there can be no exceptions. If children regularly control their own bedtimes, evenings soon become full of struggles, and morning wake-ups feel impossible. The children soon describe themselves as "night people," and the parents describe themselves as "always tired" people.

At age three-and-a-half, changing your son's sleep habits is relatively easy. However, if you don't take that important step now, your son may take charge of your evenings for many long nights ahead.

Six-Year-Old Sleeps with Mother

I have a divorced friend who allows her six-year-old son to sleep with her and has done so since he was small. I know this is inappropriate, and I'd like to tell her, but I don't know how to do this without offending her. Any suggestions?

Hardly ever should six-year-olds be sleeping in their parents' beds; of course, there are some exceptions. It's all right if there is a thunderstorm or if her son has an occasional nightmare. It's all right if he's not feeling well or if he climbs into bed with her on a weekend morning. However, it is not all right if it becomes a regular sleeping pattern because her son says he can't sleep without her. An adult and child sleeping together on a regular basis is too controlling, too overprotective, and too intimate. Under some circumstances, it may also be too sexual.

Most parents initiate the pattern of sleeping with a child in an attempt to help the child feel more secure during a difficult period, such as during or after an illness or divorce. They and the child are feeling the trauma of the illness or divorce, and sleeping together feels safe.

Unfortunately, that need for sleep security may become a habit. When Mom or Dad want to leave the bed, the child awakens and begs, whines, or cries for the parent to stay. Mom or Dad feel needed and believe they are providing the love they are committed to giving to that helpless child so warmly and contentedly snuggled in their arms. It is this commitment to love that imprisons them in that bed, but their child's dependence and insecurity increase the longer the sleep pattern continues.

The days become weeks, the weeks become months, and the months become years. Mom or Dad then find that their six-year-old, or even preadolescent, is unable to sleep without them. Sometimes the parent becomes so comfortable in the sleep relationship that even a spouse's relationship does not feel as intimate and close. More often the parent feels torn between the child's apparent requirement for security and his or her own need for adult privacy and intimacy. If a single parent becomes involved with another adult, she feels torn between the potential new partner and the child. The child expresses fears, rejection, and loneliness and pulls at the heartstrings of the parent. Now we have a dilemma that the parent could never have predicted the first night of the bedtime partnership, and it is one that is not easily resolved.

In my clinical practice, it usually takes only a simple explanation from me to the children who have this problem, in the presence of their parents. I say to the children that since they are growing up, it is time to learn to sleep alone. I explain that their parents will not sleep with them anymore, and it will be better that way. They will feel more grown up. Children usually nod their heads in agreement, although a painful tear often slips down a cheek. Children always seem to understand the appropriateness of what I've explained and usually express tenuous confidence in their ability to sleep alone.

The most difficult part is convincing the parents not to sleep with the children again. After a night or so, children always learn to sleep on their own. Sometimes they complain about difficulty falling asleep, but that hardly ever lasts long. The parents are happier and freer to have normal adult relationships, and the children are free to become more independent. It is a difficult ritual to break but easier than parents would believe and so much healthier for children.

Now, of course, comes the question of how you can communicate this information to your friend without offending her, particularly since she hasn't asked for your advice. I suggest you explain that you're concerned about her and would feel guilty if you didn't share my column with her. Don't ask her to read the column immediately nor should you ask her opinion of it. Leave the information with her but don't bring up the topic again unless your friend asks about it. In that way, you'll have provided her with information without pressuring her to follow through.

In some ways, your role is very much like mine. We can give helpful information, but we both need to leave it to our friends to decide whether or not they wish to implement our suggestions.

Closet Sleeper

My two-year-old son does not like to stay in his bed at night. He doesn't leave his room, but we find him sleeping elsewhere in the room besides the bed—even in his closet.

It is puzzling to observe how well some two-year-olds make the transition from crib to bed and how others seem to struggle with the adjustment. Your son's transition seems to be a minor problem since he stays in his room. I suggest you fasten the closet door, and let him fall asleep on the floor if he prefers. Before you go to sleep, return him to his bed without waking him. He'll soon adjust comfortably, but until then, he's safe on the floor, and you're avoiding an unnecessary power struggle. These are the terrific twos. Enjoy his new independence.

Child Displaces Stepdad in Bed

My friend has a twenty-seven-month-old daughter, who has a beau-
tiful new bedroom but refuses to sleep in her own bed. She sleeps
with her mom and her mom's new husband. Sometimes the hus-
band is asked to sleep on the couch. When the child visits her bio-
logical dad on weekends, she sleeps in his bed with him. Is this good
for the child as she grows older?

You're accurate in your observation that this two-year-old in
her parents' bed is causing a problem for her mother and stepdad.
She is clearly preventing a normal marital relationship between
them. Resentment on the part of a husband who's been displaced
from his wife's bed will certainly cause bad feelings between husband and wife. Furthermore, the stepdad may legitimately feel resentment toward the little girl, who would thrive better if they
could build a close relationship.

Cultural and individual standards differ on the benefits of children sleeping independently. It is my position that a continuous
parent-child bed relationship is too intimate and too dependent
for a child, particularly in a culture where we'd like to bring young
men and women up to know that it is possible to sleep alone. We
have far too many adolescent boys and girls believing that they
must share their beds. Sleeping alone contributes to independence
and resilience in a society where these qualities are critical to a
reasonable adult life.

19

Toilet Training and Bed-Wetting

Questions about toilet training are indeed more frequently asked than almost any other, perhaps because this developmental issue is most frustrating to parents. Parents should realize that toilet training is a major step in children's establishment of autonomy. Toilet training takes place anywhere between the age of eighteen months and five years. Both extremes are rare and the most common time for toilet training is between ages two and four. Dry diapers for two to three hours are the most important indication of readiness. Requests to use the potty should also be followed up, although the requests may only signal bids to be like Mommy or Daddy or to get attention and may give parents false hopes.

Initiating Toilet Training

Patience, patience, and more patience are your most important allies. Introduce your child to a low potty chair by taking his diaper off and having him sit on the chair. Boys' chairs will require a deflector to avoid unwanted parent showers. You can exaggerate facial expressions that may fit with your using the toilet, and some parents find that running the water in the sink is inspiring. Adult demonstrations may help, but mainly you require a combination of good timing and a little luck. Reading to your child while he is on the potty will keep him sitting patiently for a while. Don't expect performance the first time, even if he's asked to use the potty. However, if and when your child accidently urinates or has a bowel movement in it, you can hug and praise him enthusiastically. He'll likely get the idea and may ask again, or at least you can keep trying to put him on the potty every two to three hours. If your child resists, take a break for several weeks and try again. The resistance signals that the child isn't quite ready.

Public libraries have many books, videos, and even dolls you can borrow to help answer questions about toilet training and add some fun to the toilet-training process.

Using disposable pull-ups is more convenient for you than diapers while toilet training, but cotton training pants are more likely to permit your child to feel the connections between the process of toileting and the outcome (wet or soiled pants). Summer is an easier time to train children because clothes are less cumbersome and it's simpler to cope with the mess. A little urine on the grass doesn't have to be cleaned up like the stain on your carpet, and the child still has the wet pants to help him know that he could have used his nice potty.

Regression

The most frustrating parts of toilet training are the initial point before your child has the idea and the regression that sometimes happens after you were sure your child already had the idea. Returning to pants wetting seems to happen with even the slightest stress: a cold, a new preschool or child-care provider, a trip by Mom or Dad, a move to a new home, and, most common of all, the arrival of a new brother or sister. Some of these are far from slight stresses for children, yet starting from scratch tends to cause major anxiety in parents. Starting over patiently is the only alternative.

Rewards

Stickers and stars may be helpful for initiating toilet training, and small toys may accelerate the process. I helped train one grandson very rapidly on less than ten dollars' worth of small toy trucks. We called that game "pee for trucks." Obviously, readiness must come first or all the toys in the world won't work, nor is it necessary to do any major toy investing to successfully train your preschooler.

Bowel Movement Training

Bladder training almost always happens before bowel training and sometimes it seems to take children a long time to get over the fear of having their first bowel movement in the toilet. Surprisingly, some children prefer to use an adult toilet for bowel training. Perhaps it gets their mess a little farther from their bodies, or they like the funny noise as their feces hits the water with a splash. You can expect almost any variation. Small prizes may really be important to get your child to that first bowel movement in the toilet. However, after the first success, others are likely to follow automatically without the continued frustration or the prizes.

Nighttime Training

Nighttime training may immediately follow daytime training, or night urination or bed-wetting may continue a long time for your child. It's related to physical readiness and genetics rather than anything you're doing right or wrong. Stickers and stars may help with nighttime training, but scolding and punishments only seem to add more stress to an already tension-provoking problem. There are no easy answers, just more patience.

Consulting Your Pediatrician

You should certainly discuss any concerns about late training with your child's pediatrician. Sometimes urinary infections or other health problems may be involved. Night bed-wetting often runs in families, so you may wish to remember back to your own childhood nights or to those of your siblings or spouse. That may not give you reassurance but will at least prevent you from putting more pressure on your bed-wetting child. You'll remember that you didn't wet your bed on purpose, and you'll also recall the embarrassment you may have felt, which will surely keep you patient. No children enjoy wetting their beds, nor do they wet their beds to spite their parents.

One unfortunate stress for parents is that many preschools will not accept children who are not toilet trained. Unfortunately, there is little to be done about this problem except to try to train your child or select another preschool. For parents who have been procrastinating about the ordeal of training, preschool attendance could become a suitable motivator.

Some people blame the competitive aspect of parenting for the stress that surrounds toilet training. They claim parents brag when they toilet train their children early. Personally, I think it has little to do with a contest and much more to do with the delightful idea that soon you may be done with those messy diapers; and who wouldn't be eager for that completed stage? Hooray!

Summary Advice

- Don't begin toilet training too early.
- Be patient and consistent.
- Expect three steps: day bladder, day bowel, then night control.
- Use stickers or small prizes as helpful rewards.
- Avoid making toilet training into a battle.

Boy Regresses

I am the mother of a three-year-old boy who was potty-trained relatively easily at age two and a half. Six months later, however, he began wetting his pants at the baby-sitter's during the day and, shortly thereafter, at home during the evenings. I spoke to him calmly and explained that he has to use the potty and praised him excessively when he was successful, but that didn't work. Soliciting the help of family and friends, I was advised that he was just being lazy, and I considered an emotional situation. I tracked the date on which he began having "accidents" to recall what was happening during that time period. I had actually been laid off then for about a month and was spending more time with him than I had ever been able to before, so I was baffled.

I decided that perhaps there was a physiological reason for it. So we went to the doctor, but she felt it was an emotional rather physical cause. I was back to square one.

Everyone's telling me I should go ahead and put a diaper on him, so as not to make it an idle threat when he goes in his pants in the future. I would like my method to be as constructive as possible. I also don't want him to begin liking the convenience of the diaper.

I believe my son's wetting could be laziness, but I believe it could also be willful. When I think he looks like he has to go, sometimes I carry him to the bathroom, but he protests. Then when he goes in his pants a little, he'll run in the bathroom and go in the toilet. Interestingly, he does not wet the bed at night, and he does all bowel movements in the potty.

I am a single parent, and my son is my world. I want to do everything right for him, but after trying both ends of the spectrum and everything in between, I am beside myself. I hope you can help.

Probably nothing is more frustrating than having your child regress in the toilet-training process when you had full confidence that he was trained. You've done a thorough job of examining all potential psychological reasons for your son's regression. Your doctor is probably correct in pronouncing your son's regression as emotional, but it's so normal a problem that it's important you not blame either your son or yourself. Your son simply requires a re-training period. The good news is that it's likely to be brief.

Regretfully, you probably should restore the diapers, but not as a punishment, and not at night, because he obviously does not need them then. Explain to your son that he may only need them briefly and you'll remove them soon. If he's upset, tell him you'll give him a few days to show you if he can manage without them. If not, put the diapers on for a little while until he's ready to try again. Help him to put a star on the calendar for every day he has no accidents. When he has twenty dry days (they don't have to be in a row), he can earn an agreed-upon prize. Because he goes to the potty immediately after he feels himself urinating, I believe he will soon be retrained.

Try not to overreact by scolding or rushing him to the potty, and don't assume he's lazy. It's most important that your son doesn't hear you talking to other adults about the problem. That's only likely to turn the toilet training into a power struggle or make him feel as though he has no control over the problem.

Stuttering and Regression

I work in a day-care center. There is a two-year-old I've taken care of in the last few months who has started to stutter and then stopped speaking altogether. She has also ceased to be potty-trained. What can I do about this?

Neither stuttering nor regression of potty-training would be considered a problem for a two-year-old by themselves, but when a child discontinues talking, the constellation of these behaviors takes on a different meaning. Your toddler student is likely telling you she feels some kind of stress. It could be related to separation from parents, sharing attention with other children at home or in day care, or any other unusual circumstances in her little life. If you can identify the stressor and remove it, or do something to help the toddler cope with it, her problems may be over. However, if you can't discover an obvious cause after discussing the regression with her parents, recommend that they check with her pediatrician. Sometimes, however, the stresses are so minor that the child you're caring for will return to normal behavior even before you've had time to identify a cause. If so, there is surely no need for further concern.

20

Traveling with Your Preschooler

The geographic mobility of our nation has expanded travel even for preschool children; from neighborhood visits requiring only a little preparation to long automobile trips and airline travel. By age five, children are allowed to travel as unaccompanied minors on airlines, and some fly quite happily to visit a parent or grandparents. Preparation at all levels makes travel a happier experience for children, their parents, and other travelers who share the same mode of transportation.

Automobile Travel

The automobile continues to be the most common means of travel for families with preschool youngsters. For preschoolers up to the age of four there should be no other choice but sitting in a safety-approved car seat. After age four, seat belts are a must, but the front seat is no longer an alternative for children traveling in cars that have air bags.

Children do get restless in the confinement of a car seat. Whether trips are short or long, the timing of your trip seems to contribute to the comfort of the trip for everyone. If the trip is only a short one to visit a friend, family member, or neighbor, rested children probably travel best, only because they're not cranky. Furthermore, if children are not rested, they tend to fall asleep in a moving car. Fifteen minutes is hardly enough for a nap, and they are likely to be only partially rested when you reach your destination. You can keep your children busy for a short ride by observing trucks or shops along the way, listening to children's music on cassette tapes, singing children's songs, or just chatting about the visit.

Longer car rides require the opposite approach. You can hope to tire your children out before your trip by giving them extra running around time or planning much of the trip for when they usually nap or sleep. Potty breaks or diaper-changing breaks will be necessary approximately every two to three hours during the day. Use the breaks for some active running around, if possible. Surprises tucked away in separate bags can be opened every few hours on a long trip. The bags may contain toys that can be played with in the car as well as some surprise healthy snacks. Stories on tapes and even videotapes (a VCR hooked up to a cigarette lighter) can help to shorten the trip. Following are some other play tips for car trips:

Tips for Long Car Trips

- **Tell stories.** Each person tells a few sentences of the story and the story passes to the next person.
- **Play alphabet games.** Find letters of the alphabet or words on road signs.
- **Play counting games.** Count the stop signs, the number of blue cars, red cars, etc.
- **Play color games.** "I see something red. Do you see something red?" (Best in traffic)

Courtesy of Sara Rimm-Kaufman

The easiest time to travel long distances with preschool children is at night, when they're asleep. A good novel on tape can keep the driver concentrating, but it does take willing night drivers and some prearranged child care at your destination to recover from the long night drive. Children aren't always entirely rested when you arrive, but the trip is easier on the adults doing the driving.

Air Travel

Flying is a popular form of travel for family members of all ages, and air travel is usually viewed as fun for children. It is certainly easy to make a plane ride a fun excursion. Prior to your flight, encourage your children to do some running around, which seems quite natural for children old enough to walk with you, considering the distances in airports. Toddlers you carry or push in strollers will need some movement before the plane ride (or you will be desperate during the flight). Airports often have playrooms or corners with play equipment that are excellent for the climbing and sliding that little ones need before the long periods of sitting begin.

Many flights no longer offer food, and even when they do, it may be food your children would not usually choose to eat. Airplane flights are not a good time for food arguments. If you haven't brought a snack or sandwich with you, you may wish to purchase something in the airport to bring aboard. Eating also keeps your children busy, so it's a good idea for them to eat during the flight.

A trip to the restroom before the flight is a high priority. The airplane lavatory may be off-limits just when your children are in absolute need. Most airlines permit preboarding with children, and while that means extra time to be seated on the airplane, it permits you to settle in before other passengers board. It also permits you to pick up a pillow and blanket, which may encourage your children's napping. Be sure to store your children's travel bag under the seat in front of you rather than in the rack above your head. You may just need something it contains to maintain your children's peace and contentment during the flight.

There's lots to show your children outside the plane window before you take off. Equipment and machinery for preparing the plane and storing the luggage provides new vocabulary and entertainment for a preschooler. If you don't know the terminology, a visit to the library or bookstore before your trip can provide you with books that can help your children become airport experts. Even the airline attendants may be impressed, and if the flight isn't too crowded, your children may be able to meet the friendly pilot and even receive a "wings" pin.

For your children's first airplane trip, you'll want them to know what to expect when they take off, and if they're not sleeping by then, they'll need preparation for understanding the noises and feelings of the plane's takeoff and landing. If you, too, are a new traveler, ask the flight attendant. Knowing what to expect relieves the feelings of anxiety you might have if you're not sure what's normal. If your children seem anxious, reading to them, playing a game, or listening to children's music on a portable cassette recorder dissipates fears for children rather easily. If your toddler is still drinking a bottle or using a pacifier, the sucking seems to alleviate pressure in their little ears during takeoff and landing; likewise, if you're breast-feeding and don't mind the lack of privacy, the nursing will make your baby more comfortable. If your children are beyond all that and know how to chew gum, it, too, helps relieve ear pressures. Some airline attendants will supply ear covers that seem to help small children who are uncomfortable; cupping your hands over their ears also helps. Some small children don't seem to be bothered at all by the flight, so you may even wonder at these suggested precautions.

Independent Air Travel

Not every five-year-old should be traveling alone, but if your children are seasoned travelers and there's a loving and dependable family member at the end of an airplane trip to greet your young traveler, traveling alone is certainly a confidence builder for children unequaled by almost any other experience. However, independent flights are not a good idea to push on a child who doesn't feel ready or who is fearful. If the child really feels ready for a trip, and the trip doesn't involve changing airplanes, you can feel confident that the airlines will handle your child carefully and safely.

Be sure to arrive at the gate early. You'll have special paperwork to complete to assure communication and appropriate pickup. Furthermore, your child will be escorted on the plane by the attendant before others are seated. Usually you are not permitted on the plane for departure. Prepare yourself to remain calm. The idea of your child traveling alone may be more traumatic for you than it is for your child. Definitely send along favorite books or toys for the trip, if only to reassure yourself. A special surprise in the travel bag, to be opened after takeoff, will also help. A telephone call to the greeting family member after the plane is no longer in view will confirm that a loving recipient will be at the other end of the flight to hug and greet and to absolutely prove by picture identification that they are the legally correct party to accept the child. An immediate call from the person meeting the plane is important reassurance that your little traveler has arrived. After the pioneer flight, you and your child will feel much more comfortable about traveling alone, and he or she can visit a parent or grandparents more frequently.

The Well-Stocked Travel Bag

The well-stocked travel bag seems to be an essential for all kinds of travel. Items in the bag will vary depending on the age and needs of your preschooler. On page 186 are some suggestions for a travel bag.

Summary Advice

- To make your travel worry-free, plan ahead.
- Consider children's nap times.
- Encourage children to run around before flying.
- Bring snacks on airplane flights.
- Talk to your children about what to expect when flying.
- Consider permitting children to travel alone.

Well-Stocked Travel Bag

GAMES/ACTIVITIES

A favorite (but small) snugglie or toy

Small books

Small toys: Matchbox cars, pocket-size dolls, finger puppets or small hand puppets (good to have two of these for interaction; a child can play with both, or a parent and child can play; also a great way to give your child messages, by having toy/puppet "talk" to them)

Drawing supplies: especially good to have reusable ones such as Etch-a-Sketch, Magna Doodle

Paper with crayons or pencil, clipboard

Headphones with cassette player for older preschoolers who may enjoy listening to favorite music or book tapes

Travel-size games

SNACKS

Suggestions: dry cereal mix, crackers, raisins, dried fruit, string cheese, cereal bars in recloseable small containers that a child can hold (avoid salty, sticky, or crumbly foods)

Small bagels, unsalted soft pretzels, small sandwiches

Drinks in recloseable containers; juice boxes (consider water instead of juice; it makes less of a mess)

CLOTHING

Diapers or pull-ups for a younger child

Extra sweatshirt, pants, etc., packed in a Ziploc bag (squeeze out all air when closing to make a small package). Packing clothing in a bag keeps it clean and dry and provides a place to put any soiled clothing or diapers

Bibs to make eating in car less messy

MISCELLANEOUS

Moist towelettes in small container, essential for younger kids in diapers; also helpful for hands, faces, or cleaning up spills

Pocket packs of tissues

Courtesy of Janet Rimm

21

When Both Parents Have Careers

Many preschoolers live in homes where both parents work outside the home, either part or full time. In those situations, special issues beyond child care seem to surface repeatedly.

When Work Schedules Differ

Sometimes parents deliberately plan their careers in shifts so that one parent is caretaker while the other works, and vice versa. The advantages are obvious: less need for outside child care, and children are with at least one parent most of the time.

The major problem for the family with differing schedules is that there is almost no time for planning or for the adults to be together. Both parents often feel cheated of adult companionship, and instead of team cooperation the parents may unconsciously compete to be the easiest or best parent. It is harder than ever for parents to stay on the same team when they have so little time to talk about their differences in approaches to parenting. It's easier than ever for children to manipulate parents in ways that can be harmful. For example, the candy that Mom says no to is easy to get when Dad is at home, and bedtime is later with Mom than Dad because Mom reads more stories.

It is true that absolute consistency isn't necessary or possible, but some agreement on guidelines will be helpful to your children. Parents may even wish to write notes to each other, much as they do with their day-care providers. Keep a notebook handy.

Adult dates for talking about kids and just being together are required to keep a marriage and a family together when schedules don't coincide. It is important to take that advice seriously.

Guilt

Guilt is the other important issue that causes trouble for dual-career families. Although both parents sometimes feel guilty about not spending enough time with their children, mothers who may recall how much more time their own mothers spent with them are particularly vulnerable to guilt. Guilt motivates parents to buy too much for their children, to permit their children to stay up too late, and to say yes when parents know it would be healthier to say no. It would be good for parents to make absolutely *no* decisions based on guilt.

On the other hand, childhood is fleeting. In your busy plans, find appropriate quality time for your children or your guilt will follow you for the rest of your life. Too many fathers have shared their regrets with me about the little time they spent with their sons, and I expect that both mothers and father will soon be expressing regrets to their therapists about the paucity of time they made available to their children. Time is your most precious commodity, and children do require some. Lessons and classes will never substitute for your love.

Finding Help

Although dual-career families don't always manage better financially because of two salaries, they may be in a position to purchase some services that free up time to spend with their children. Start searching for help by making a list of all the chores that you or you and your spouse are required to accomplish during any one week. After your list is complete, think creatively about which of these could be accomplished more efficiently by you and which could be accomplished by a helper.

You may find that you can actually invent ways to be together as a family without too much financial sacrifice. Housecleaning, grocery shopping, laundry, errands, meal preparation, gardening, and billing services are available to shorten your own list of household chores. As your children mature, they may be able to assist in some of these tasks, but during the preschool years, you may feel inundated by chores while anxious to spend some time playing and being with your children.

Consider which chores you may be able to delegate to someone. A neighborhood teenager may be willing to do your laundry twice a week for a fee and work experience. A senior citizen friend may be searching for a way to earn a small income, and a mother who is a full-time homemaker might enjoy earning some additional income. There may be a take-home restaurant nearby where you can order an inexpensive healthy meal from time to time. Consider, too, that you may have friends and neighbors who are willing to trade services, such as trips to the dry cleaner or carpooling kids to activities. Carpooling with neighbors to drive children to lessons can also save time. All these can free you to have several extra hours with your children each week.

Career Travel

Career travel is the most difficult for parents of preschoolers to deal with, but with a small amount of planning, you can manage your career opportunities and stay in close touch with your children during your travels. Daily telephone calls can update you, and even if your children are little, they will be eager to hear your voice. If telephone time won't work, record your morning or bedtime messages on a cassette tape. Try to keep your messages cheerful. You don't want your children to dissolve into tears each time they hear your voice. You want them to know that you're thinking of them and that you're sure they'll be fine. Daily surprise notes and even small gifts can be left for them to open while thinking of you. Despite the commercialization of bringing something home for the kids, it is still a good idea to bring something home from the trip that permits you to share your travels. Even a picture postcard is sufficient to help them understand your travels better.

No Need to Apologize

Although you miss your children and may feel guilty, apologies for your work are inappropriate and confusing to children. You're doing important work. Take pride in your contribution. Let your children know you're a good role model, and you have a good work ethic. They can learn those excellent values from you, and you can relax together and have fun and can also have a successful and fulfilling career.

Summary Advice

- Differing work schedules make teamwork more difficult.
- Don't make decisions based on guilt.
- Make time with your children a high priority.
- Get help for household chores.
- Have frequent communication during career travel.
- Take pride in your work; don't apologize for it.

Not Enough Time

Both my husband and I are professionals-in-training. Our jobs require many long hours away from home. We are blessed with a wonderful five-month-old boy but are very concerned about our lack of time with him. We have a baby-sitter who showers him with attention and affection, and when we are home, we almost exclusively spend our time playing with him.

Please advise us about what we can do to help our child feel loved and secure despite our time away from him. Also, are there any studies that show adverse effects on children in this type of situation?

Strangely enough, I think it's possible that you may be giving your son *too much* attention. Although five-month-old babies do require a great deal of love and care, they don't need every moment of your time when you get home. It's even possible, by your description, that your baby-sitter may also be "showering" your son with too much attention and affection.

While five-month-old babies should have their share of stimulation, they also require time to play quietly alone with a crib toy or their hands and feet. They should even have opportunities to look around them at whatever catches their eye. Too much stimulation and attention can lead them to dependency upon attention, and later, they may not be willing to play alone at all.

You should certainly spend some quality time with your son each night, but just as certainly, not all night. You need rest, and so does your son.

Perhaps you require only the reassurance that effective child-care providers don't traumatize children of working parents. If both of you give him a reasonable amount of attention in the evening, your son will feel loved and rested, and so will his parents.

Mother of Infant Travels Frequently

I live in Alaska, and I work out of the city every other week at the oil fields. I've been doing this since my son was four months old. I worry that I should be home more with him, especially when he begins school. Am I traumatizing him?

Since you have been functioning this way for so long, and your husband has been with your son, who seems to be doing quite well, you don't really need to worry about traumatizing him. It sounds as if he's made a good adjustment to spending some time with both you and his dad. As long as there is consistency between his loving parents, there should be only the few normal problems.

As he gets older, you can stay in close touch with him through daily telephone conversations or letters. He'll soon be able to keep a daily journal of all his activities to share with you. That way you won't feel like you're missing out on so much of his growing up, and he'll feel very close to both you and his dad.

When school begins, you'll surely want to ask him about school, and let him know how important his education is to you. Mom, I think it must be hardest of all for you, but thanks to you and a loving dad, your son sounds very secure.

22

Nontraditional Families

T here are so many forms of nontraditional families in our society that I could easily write an entire book on special issues related to any or all of these. For the purpose of this book, I'll emphasize the communication issues related to preschoolers because we know that communication about unusual circumstances is often postponed and causes difficulties for young people later in life. It's important to remember that preschoolers have limitations in their understanding, and their questions can help guide you in deciding how much to tell them.

Adopted Children

Adoption is so common in our society that adopted children can easily understand that they are not the only children who have been adopted. Indeed, if parents adopt several children, they feel comfortable with sharing information about their children's adoption early. Parents have the most difficulty explaining to a first child who is adopted at birth about adoption.

Around age four is a good time to explain adoption to your preschooler, because four-year-olds are able to differentiate real from the imaginary. However, you don't have to wait until that age. Instead, you can use a teaching opportunity like a friend's or relative's pregnancy to describe how babies grow inside a mommy. You can then also explain to your child that he or she grew inside a mommy, too, but that it was not you or your spouse. You can further share how you searched for parents who couldn't take care of a baby and wanted someone to love and care for that baby for them. The rest of the story can provide information of how lucky you were to find parents who would share their baby with you, or some other appropriate way of explaining your love. If your child asks questions about his other parents, don't hesitate to answer in simple terms. If not, save other explanations for other teaching opportunities, such as exposure to other adopted children or other pregnant mothers.

Preliminary research indicates that open adoption, where birth parents stay in contact with adoptive parents and their children, is effective and has not caused problems. However, I would not recommend it to either the birth or adoptive parents. I believe it has the potential for being confusing to children to have two sets of parents before they are old enough to have learned basic values. Of course, this is an individual decision that should be thought out carefully by both sets of parents before an adoption takes place.

Foster Children

Unlike adoption, foster parenting is usually understood as a temporary role, and foster children often know as soon as they are aware that they have two sets of parents. Foster parents, who love and care for these children, need to be cautious to leave a primary role for the birth parents, who often visit the children regularly. They also need to have some privacy for talking to the parents about the children's progress and about their own approach to parenting. If the parents are able to care for the children for short periods of time alone by taking walks or playing together, or even for overnight visits, communication about children's routines needs to be shared and preferably written down, so that the routines are not disrupted. Foster children require positive preparation for a parent's visit and should hear respectful descriptions of their parents. That may be more difficult than it seems, as these parents sometimes have serious physical or mental health problems or may be dealing with drug and alcohol abuse, which preschoolers can't really understand. Describing these problems as general illnesses is sufficient for preschoolers. If parents have poor parenting skills, it's important not to criticize them in front of their children, or the children will not learn to trust their parents.

If parents regain custody of their children after they have been in foster placement, it is important for the parents to speak respectfully about the foster parents and continue to visit or stay in contact with them. Parents often find this difficult because the foster parents may seem like a threat to them. They may fear their children will love their foster parents more if contact continues. Preschoolers will remember their foster parents who loved them and will feel deprived of their love. They will make comparisons with their parents and may even feel angry at their parents if they can't visit with their foster parents. As the children feel more secure with their birth parents, visits to foster parents can decrease, but it may be an enriching relationship that can continue during the children's lives if parents and foster parents are respectful of one another and if foster parents can stand back from the relationship appropriately. As you can see, the difficult emotional issues here often require individual and careful management.

Multiples

Multiple children, including twins, triplets, and more, are common in a generation that has used various approaches to encouraging fertility. Although the guidance given for all preschoolers applies to multiple children within the family as well, there are a few special concerns Multiples often develop specialized relationship with each other that become so comfortable that parents avoid involving them with other children. It's obviously more difficult to arrange play groups and playdates for two or three children when it's so apparent they've learned to keep each other company. It's true multiples do learn some social skills automatically, like sharing and taking turns; nevertheless, it is perhaps even more important that they are exposed to other children, both singly and in combination, to prepare them for the real world of school where they will have opportunities to be both separate and together.

Interestingly enough, even identicals often develop different personalities, with one becoming more dominant and the other more dependent. It is often the older one (by as little as twenty seconds) that takes on the more dominant role. Much like siblings, rivalry provides them each with a niche within the family, which only emphasizes the importance of their developing social skills with other children. Their set relationship can become too comfortable, and all children need the balance of learning assertiveness and sharing with others.

If Father Is the Homemaker

The nurturance, security, and enrichment preschool children need can be provided by either parent. There are many families in which mothers are full-time professionals and breadwinners while fathers take on the responsibility of full-time homemaker.

I have observed only a few problems with this arrangement. Because of the reversal of roles, mothers who don't have as much time with their children and feel guilty tend to want to correct and instruct the father in parenting, either to the extent of diminishing the father's confidence or adversely affecting the children's confidence in their father. Also, fathers who do full-time fathering at home sometimes lack other male companionship and feel awkward when surrounded by other parents who are mostly women. The role is unclear both for the dad and for the other women. Sometimes dads who are at home full days do more roughhousing with children than moms would normally do and that can generalize to the playground (see chapter 3).

Finally, as children mature and need Dad less, fathers, much like mothers, tend to want to hold on to their parenting role, sometimes becoming overprotective, criticizing their wives for putting in too many hours at work, and losing confidence in their ability to move into a career other than parenting. In other words, dads who are full-time homemakers often have some of the transitional problems that mothers who are full-time homemakers have. They need to develop interests and careers as their children mature to keep their family relationships and their confidence growing.

Mother-Led Families

If you've had a child outside of marriage or you've been divorced, ideally, full father involvement and respect for you provides the best environment for your child. However, if your preschooler's father did not marry you and never became involved with your child, you may be in a better position than if there has been a difficult divorce or a father who was uncertain about his relationship to you and your child. The most difficult problem for children is the insecurity of feeling the uneven love or rejection of a father who wants to be involved some of the time but is not reliable. The father who brings big gifts but provides no regular support is simply unexplainable to a preschooler. The father who is mean or disrespectful to a mother does great harm to children.

Here are some ways you can explain father relationships to your preschooler depending on the situation:

You have a real daddy, but he wasn't quite ready to be a daddy, so he said it was better for me to take care of you.

You had another daddy, but he had to travel far away, and I married the daddy you have now. He loves you very much, and he will always be your real daddy (if adoptive).

Your daddy comes to visit you when he can, but Mommy can take good care of you all the time.

Your daddy got very sick and died. He would have loved you very much, and you would have loved him, too. (Use this description only if it's true.)

Harm is only done if you tell your preschool children that their father is irresponsible, unloving, selfish, or unkind. You are better off saying little or nothing about a dad who is not acting appropriately. It is also harmful to tell your son he reminds you of his dad if you use that reminder in a negative way. The greatest risk for children in mother-led families is to hear only negative stories about males and fathers. For little girls, it may cause a mistrust and fear of men; for little boys, it may lead to lack of confidence in personal masculinity and rebellion toward mother and all of mother's other positive messages. By adolescence, a gang can become a tempting outlet.

If your husband has died, and you make the comparison in a positive way, it can be helpful to your children. The risk of using a deceased father as a role model is that there may be such a tendency to idealize the father that, as a boy gets older, he may feel as though he can never live up to his idealized father's expectations. However, this can be corrected as children mature and is not an issue during the preschool years.

A risk mentioned earlier in single-parent homes is that of overempowering the oldest child and treating that child in a too-adult manner. Even as a preschooler, the child will begin to expect "equal rights" with a parent, which may cause the child problems in preschool or at home. It will cause major problems for the parent if she decides to remarry. The child may feel rejected and have difficulty accepting a father who reduces the child's status. It's important for a single mom to keep some adult life to herself and not include children in all activities, and especially not in her bed on a regular basis.

Learning about fathers and men, in general, is important in households that are led by single mothers. Books and stories can help you to provide the dad dimension to your children's lives. Movies and television can be helpful, too, if you are selective, and Boy Scouts and Big Brothers are important for many boys, whether or not they have a father at home.

If There Is Only a Father

Due to divorce or death, many single-parent families are now led by fathers. If they are good role models, boys can look to them for achievement and confidence. Daughters can learn to relate to males comfortably. Lacking, nevertheless, will be a suitable female role model to help girls have confidence in their femininity and to allow sons a comfortable emotional relationship with girls and women. Of course, schools provide many appropriate role models because teachers are predominantly female. Negativity toward women or children's mothers, however, is equally harmful to children whether they are boys or girls. Excellent child care is especially important when the father's career limits time spent with children.

When Grandparents Do the Parenting

If a child is born outside of marriage or there is a death or divorce, grandparents often become more involved in parenting than typical grandparents. They can, of course, provide excellent parenting to their grandchildren, and this book is written for them as well. However, difficulties can crop up if the mother marries or decides to take over parenting again. Grandparents feel strongly bonded to their grandchildren and vice versa. Mothers often have mixed feelings, both needing and wanting the help, but resenting the priority role their own parents have with their children. The emergencies that precipitate such arrangements have often left little time for rational discussion and planning, and children may feel caught in the middle.

The courts are beginning to fill with custody suits about grandparent rights. There is obviously not one solution to this problem, as there is not one cause of such a situation. I bring this to your attention so you can understand how strained relationships can become for families under these difficult circumstances. The best advice I can give is to plan ahead and not wait until problems arise. Clear communication about the amount of help required is critical, but parents and grandparents may not be able to make these predictions for the future. An objective counselor may be able to help you to plan an appropriate strategy that can provide closeness without the friction that often permeates parent-grandparent relationships.

Divorce

Divorce is never easy for children, but under some circumstances, it is certainly better than staying in a bad or abusive marriage. Unfortunately, the worse the marriage, the more difficult the divorce is likely to be. No couple should ever get a divorce without receiving some serious counseling first. Many apparently bad marriages have been helped and corrected by counseling and have led to successful families in the future. It's important not to believe that having another baby will cure a bad marriage. It will only lead to another unhappy child.

The most important principle of divorce is to permit a child to love both parents without having to make a choice. Of course, there are exceptions to that principle when a parent no longer wants to take parenting responsibility or when there is risk of a parent being abusive. For most divorces, the better the parents adjust to the divorce, the easier it is for the children. If the two parents can remain respectful friends, children are much less likely to be traumatized. Children feel more secure if their parents can say nice things about each other even if they are no longer married to each other. You'll continue to need to be on the same parenting team.

Blending Families

Remarriages after divorce often bring together several children of similar ages. During the preschool years these children may have been "onlies" in their original family. Unlike the situation when a new baby comes into a household, when an older child is given a special role, another preschooler in the family may cause some severe sibling rivalry and extreme competition. A child who's heard "You're my special girl (or boy)" may have great difficulty allowing another child into specialness. It's important for each parent to have some one-to-one time for their own child as the children gradually learn to share attention. It's a good idea for each child also to have some one-to-one time with the stepchild in order to build some bonding. Blending of preschool families is probably not as difficult as blending families with older children, but don't expect the change to be easy.

Summary Advice

- If your child's adopted, explain between ages three and four.
- Foster parents should build bridges to children's parents when possible.
- Multiples require socialization with other children.
- Be respectful of your child's other parent in single families and after divorce.
- Full-time–homemaking dads need to develop outside interests and careers as their children mature.

(*continued*)

- If you are the only parent, find substitute role models for the absent parent.
- Careful communication can prevent problems for families being led temporarily by grandparents.
- Don't divorce without counseling.
- Don't stay in a hopelessly bad or abusive marriage.
- Families should be blended carefully to avoid extreme sibling rivalry.

One Dominant, One Submissive Twin

I have twin sons who are the youngest of four boys. One is very dominant and independent and one is very submissive. I find myself always correcting the dominant one and cuddling the submissive one. I try not to get them in those roles, but how can I stop doing this?

Parents often observe their twins in this dominant-dependent relationship. Actually, even two same-gender, close-in-age children often take on these opposite roles. Your older sons may also exhibit similar patterns, although theirs is probably less extreme. Furthermore, the patterns seem to perpetuate themselves, or at least parents tend to feel trapped into perpetuating them.

Your more dominant son needs opportunities for positive leadership so he can direct his energy and power appropriately. Try to help him develop some new interests and activities that will involve him without his brother. Some separation from each other will diminish the competition and will neutralize your son's dominance. Since his friends will be less likely to accept this bossiness, it is likely to be tempered toward more reasonable leadership.

Of course, your more dependent son will especially benefit from some separation from his overpowering brother. Separate father-son trips or activities will be helpful in building his confidence. While you should continue to be affectionate (to both your sons), do avoid overcoddling him. Although your submissive son may search out your protection and affection, continued support may serve as a vote of nonconfidence. It is like saying to him, "You need me more than your brother does," and his feelings of inadequacy may increase. The importance of encouraging interests and active involvement are even more critical for this dependent son.

All in all, as you try to balance your parenting among your four boys, expect to feel some frustration. Don't be surprised to find that a growing confidence in one may cause another to lose confidence. While you will want to continue some total family activities, do provide work and play opportunities in one-on-one, parent-child relationships.

While it surely must feel challenging and overwhelming to raise four boys in a family, I have met some wonderful families who have struggled with similar situations. Celebrate your son's individuality as well as their team work, and you can look forward to someday adding four lovely daughters-in-law to balance things out and deliver you from an all-masculine perspective.

Adapting to New Custody

I'm a psychiatrist who works with adults who have abused alcohol and drugs. One of my patients lost custody of her child because she was abusing alcohol. She's gone through treatment and is now being judged as ready to resume custody. What advice can I give her to make the transition smoother for her and her preschool daughter?

I assume your patient's daughter was in foster placement during her treatment. It wold be best for her to arrange several visits with the child before actually taking full custody. Going on a few excursions and having her at home for an afternoon or a day will help both mother and daughter make the transition. Full support by the foster parents will also be important for a positive transition. Parents and foster parents can explain it as a recovery from illness, which is accurate, but doesn't involve detail that a preschooler can't handle.

The mother would also benefit from becoming familiar with the routine her daughter has been experiencing during her foster placement. Although routines don't have to be exactly the same, if rules and expectations are fairly similar, it will help the child adjust. It will also be important to provide some counseling support to the mother as she takes over her parenting role again. It will take a little while for the mother to regain confidence in her parenting, but it's important that her daughter trust the mother in order to feel secure. Mother may need to act more confident than she feels.

Preparing Child for Divorce

How can I prepare my five-year-old son for an imminent divorce?

Your child is probably experiencing a lot of uncertainty and concern over your divorce. In particular, if you and your husband argue over issues pertaining to your son, he might feel guilty and responsible. Explain to your son that your marriage is not working, but it is not his fault. Tell him that both you and your husband love him, and just because you are getting a divorce, it doesn't mean he can't still love both of you.

Don't say negative things to him about his dad. Allow him time alone with his father. If you can, prevent him from hearing the conflicts between you and your husband.

It is important that your son doesn't become your confidant in this difficult situation. It would be easy for you to confide in him and tell him details about the situation from your perspective. Instead, this is a good opportunity for you to seek out adult family and friends who have the time and willingness to help you through this difficult period. Counseling is also almost a necessity.

Your decision to get a divorce may be very difficult for your son. However, it is likely that things will become easier for him over time, provided your conflict with his dad doesn't cause him to feel caught in the middle.

Single Man Not Ready for Fatherhood

My friend and I have just had a baby. We are just that, friends. We never planned to marry, and we never planned a baby. She'd like to marry someone else, and someday, I expect, I will, too, although I feel far from ready for marriage or fatherhood at this time. I feel bonded to my son already, but not to his mother. How can I do the right thing for my son?

You and your friend made a serious mistake, but you need to be loving parents for your son. You will probably require immediate counseling to help you determine how you can be responsible for this child in the future. First and foremost, it would be good to consider adoption. There are many loving couples who are searching for a healthy child to adopt.

If your friend wants to keep your son and you do not, you will at least be required to share the financial responsibility for him. If your friend wants to marry a man who would like to adopt your son, that would remove your financial obligation and permit your son to grow up with a loving father and mother, both who apparently feel ready to parent.

If you decide you want to take full financial and emotional responsibility for your son, you should carefully think through your decision before your bonding becomes too strong. A good father must be a good father forever, not only for two or three years. A good father must be totally dependable and should be respectful toward his son's mother. These requirements continue even after you are married to another woman and have other children. Your infant son will not feel rejected if he is adopted and loved by other parents or another father at this age, but he will suffer terribly if you leave him after having been close to him for several years. He will truly feel rejected, and he doesn't deserve to suffer. This whole issue is far more complex than a night of making love, and I know by your question that you want to make a careful and caring decision.

Tips for Stay-at-Home Dad

I am a thirty-four-year-old father of two who is about to become the main caregiver (Mr. Mom). I was hoping you might have some tips for "stay-at-home" dads.

It should be comforting for you to know that you are not alone, but it will be even more comforting if you can find a few other stay-at-home dads in the neighborhood with whom you can exchange problems and solutions. Stay-at-home moms have supported each other for years, and you may feel a bit bored and lonely with only the company of your children.

If you think of yourself as a teacher, it will help you to structure your children's day. Allow time for family play at home, rest, meals, reading, individual time with each child, social time with other children, and some quiet time for yourself. It will take some strategy, but actual planning of your day will prevent your children from controlling you. Incidentally, such plans can never be rigid because children are never entirely predictable.

One other small problem I've discovered for stay-at-home dads is that they tend to do more roughhousing and teasing with their children than moms do. Unfortunately, this roughhousing often generalizes to the preschool classroom and may cause some behavior problems, especially for high energy children. An appropriate guide for play with your children is to play outside as they will be expected to play on school playgrounds, and play more quietly indoors as they would be expected to play in school.

Welcome to the home workplace. There will be many more joys then trials, and I admire your courage.

23

Getting Ready for Kindergarten

Children fortunate enough to attend a high-quality preschool or child-care program ... have a better chance of achieving to high levels than those who do not.

Carnegie Task Force Report,
1996

Kindergarten may seem like a small step for children who have attended a good preschool or day-care program, but it is nevertheless a huge psychological step for parents and a major transition for your children. Although children who are familiar with the learning routines of preschool don't have to adapt as much as children who have not attended any preschool classes, kindergarten will seem exciting and a step in maturation for all children.

Pre-Kindergarten Assessment

Children are often registered and introduced to kindergarten in the spring before kindergarten actually begins. Many schools conduct assessments in the spring as well, while others may conduct their assessments before school begins in the fall or within the kindergarten classroom after school has begun. The following skills lists include some readiness skills for kindergarten that are often tested in prekindergarten assessments. If the results are given beforehand and there are weak areas, parents are able to get the help their children would benefit from over the summer. Sometimes schools will simply assure parents that their child is ready without further details, and no additional information is necessary.

If recommendations are made for specific activities that you can provide for your child during the summer, it's a good idea to spend a little time each day working with your child on them. It's important not to feel anxious about the identified problems, or you may find yourself putting pressure on your child. Sometimes suggestions will be made that surprise you because you are sure your child is competent in the specified area. Review the material with your child anyway, just to be certain. It may only be that your child was not at her best the day of the screening or was hesitant with strangers. That would not be unusual, and teachers realize that pre-kindergarten assessment results aren't always reliable. In most cases, however, these assessments are helpful to your children.

Delayed Entrance to Kindergarten

If children's birthdays are near the kindergarten entrance deadline, parents may be in a quandary about whether to hold them back a year or request early entrance to school. Research indicates that for most children the best advice is to follow the school district guidelines for entrance to kindergarten. In other words, counter to the belief of many parents and teachers, the concept of holding capable children back a year has not proven effective. It does not help children's achievement or social adjustment. Holding back bright children is less likely to provide them with the challenge they should be meeting in school. For children who

Typical Readiness Skills for Kindergarten

READING READINESS
Knows letters of the alphabet
Knows some nursery rhymes
Prints and recognizes own first name
Can tell a story from pictures

LISTENING
Pays attention
Follows simple directions
Retells a simple story in sequence

SIMPLE RELATIONSHIP CONCEPTS
Understands big, little; long, short; more, less; in, out; top, bottom; front, back; hot, cold; over, under

COLORS AND SHAPES
Recognizes primary colors
Knows triangles, circles, squares, rectangles

NUMBERS
Counts to ten
Counts objects

MOTOR SKILLS
Walks a straight line
Hops, jumps, and marches
Throws a ball
Pastes pictures on paper
Completes simple puzzles (five pieces)
Handles scissors
Cuts and draws simple shapes
Controls pencil and crayons

SOCIAL-EMOTIONAL DEVELOPMENT
Knows first and last name, parents' names, home address, and telephone number
Expresses self verbally
Can be away from parents for three hours
Dresses self
Gets along with children
Shares with others
Works independently
Maintains self-control
Recognizes authority

have more difficulty learning, it may, in fact, deprive them of a year of important learning. However, if a recommendation is made for your child to wait a year before entering school, you will want to request additional information. If the reason given is only that "young children do better when held back" and your child has no skills deficits, this stereotype is not good advice to follow.

If the advice suggests your child is immature but is intellectually ready, there is a great likelihood that your child will catch up in maturity in a short time, However, if there are skills deficits or if your child seems to have below average ability, you may want to ask for a further evaluation by the school psychologist. If the continued recommendation is to hold the child back a year, it's important that your child gets a strong academic enrichment program for the year prior to kindergarten in an appropriate preschool environment. Don't assume that a year at home will provide the appropriate enrichment.

Early Entrance to Kindergarten

If you're considering early entrance to kindergarten for your child because he has just missed the deadline or because he's showing advanced skills, you should go for a professional evaluation on whether or how you should attempt to enter him into school early. States and even separate school districts vary in their policies about early admission to kindergarten. Research shows that intellectually gifted children (with IQs above 130), who are also screened for social and emotional maturity, do benefit from early entrance and do adjust well socially. Variations are related to both the individual child and the particular school. This does not suggest that all bright children are candidates for early entrance to school, however. It is a decision that should be made cautiously, on an individual basis.

Preparation for Kindergarten

All children benefit from some preparation for kindergarten. Children who have not attended preschool could benefit from "playing school" at home with parents or older siblings. Reading to children is always beneficial, but you may wish to increase the reading time prior to entrance to kindergarten to encourage your children's increased span of attention. Listening to stories on tapes without a book or listening to appropriate radio programs, like *Rabbit Ears Radio* on public radio, can increase children's listening skills. Printing letters, completing dot-to-dot pictures, drawing and coloring, and accomplishing cut-and-paste projects all help to hone small muscle coordination skills. Teaching children to follow directions will also help them adjust to kindergarten.

Here are some additional tips for parents for their children's entrance to kindergarten:

Additional Tips for Getting Ready for Kindergarten

- Participate in all the orientation activities the school offers for children.
- Visit the school; meet other children and their parents.
- Children make a smoother adjustment to school if they have at least one friend in the classroom. Check with your child's new teacher to see who will be in the class. Arrange a playdate with a child who will be in your child's class.
- If your child has attended a preschool, encourage your child's preschool teacher to talk to the kindergarten teacher before school begins.
- Talk to your child about the new expectations of his or her kindergarten teacher. Children will be expected to sit still and listen, raise their hand when they want to talk, and take turns receiving the teacher's attention.
- Teach your child social skills to meet new people; for example, "Hi, my name is Emily. What's yours?" Encourage them to participate in the classroom.
- Kindergarten classrooms are designed to encourage parent participation. Talk to your child's teacher about volunteering in the classroom.
- Stay in close contact with your child's teacher through phone calls or notes.

Courtesy of Sara Rimm-Kaufman

The most important preparation of all is in the area of attitude. If you communicate to children that they will thoroughly enjoy kindergarten and that they will also love learning, they're likely to be off to a good educational and emotional start.

Summary Advice

- Follow advice given after pre-kindergarten screening.
- Expect an individual evaluation for delayed or early entrance.
- Prepare children for kindergarten skills.
- Prepare children for social adjustment.
- Be positive about school.

Holding Back Capable Kindergartner

Our daughter is a very young kindergartner and her teacher has suggested that she is immature and should be held out a year so that she will fit in better. However, she has been reading since she was four and can count to 100 and do simple addition and subtraction. We worry that holding her back will cause her boredom in later years, but we don't want her to feel too pressured, either.

You have good reason to be puzzled and concerned. Your first step is to request an evaluation by your school psychologist or a local private psychologist who specializes in evaluating gifted children. Step two is to ask the teacher to describe your daughter's immature behaviors.

If your child tests in the very superior IQ range, she may be better off being young in the class. Research in the field of gifted children continually finds that children who are accelerated or entered early usually do better with the additional challenge.

Girls tend to mature earlier than boys. Sometimes symptoms of immaturity are indicative that a child has not been given enough independence. These same symptoms may also mean a child has been given too much power. You would be able to know that better after the teacher describes the problems.

Gifted children often adjust better to older children than children of the same age. The test results and parent and teacher observations of the child's adjustment for three or four months will help you to make better decisions for her future.

Separating Triplets in Kindergarten

I have four-year-old triplets—two girls and one boy. I will have them in a three- and four-year-old group at preschool again this year. As triplets, they tend to keep to themselves and do not really assert themselves. Last year, I helped out half the school year, but I think I may not this year so they won't have anyone to cling to. My question is: When they enter kindergarten, should I keep them together or separate them?

If it is at all possible to keep the children in separate classes, I highly recommend it. It will help your children to develop independence. They have considerable time together at home to build a close sibling relationship, but multiples can become either too dependent on one another or too competitive if they are always together.

As to your volunteering at school, it will surely not hurt for you to help out on occasions, but it is better not to be there on a daily basis. Special pressures and special joys accompany the parenting of multiples. Triple good wishes to you on your parenting voyage.

Difficulty with Change

My four-and-a-half-year-old son has problems with change. He was in nursery school five afternoons a week. He would cry anytime the class situation changed a little—for example, if one of his teachers was absent or they went to a different classroom. He will be entering kindergarten in September, and I'm concerned about how he will do. His nursery school teachers were very nurturing, but I can't picture them to be that way next year. How can I help him to cope with changes?

The good news is that his kindergarten teacher is also likely to be supportive. It is always helpful to give children a brief, positive notice of a change to come and then to assume positively that they'll adjust. It may help to give your son change experiences for practice rather than avoid change for fear he'll cry. For example, a new baby-sitter or an experience with Dad or Grandmom alone will help him build confidence in his ability to cope with changes. Of course, your son will need a little more support and encouragement than some other children might, but he also needs your vote of confidence that he can handle transitions.

24

Grandparents Are Important

If your children are fortunate enough to have grandparents who are alive to love and be loved by, it's worth making the effort to build that relationship that ties generations together. With the increase of two-career families as well as working grandparents today, family busyness may make it harder than ever for families to visit or vacation together. Even if visits are shorter than they used to be, the efforts are worthwhile. Shorter visits can sometimes actually be more successful than long ones. They may be over before tension builds, and their very brevity may encourage everyone to make greatest effort and value the time together.

Grandparents as Caretakers

If grandparents are regular caretakers or live in the neighborhood, communication guidelines need to be more detailed, as discussed in chapter 11. However, good family relations, especially in very close conditions, are worth pursuing. Of course, the same holds true for aunts, uncles, and cousins if you're fortunate to have them living nearby.

Sometimes grandparents can even provide their adult children with a much wished-for reprieve from parenting by caring for grandchildren temporarily. For the many working grandparents, free time may be scarce, and child care may not be possible. One-at-a-time visits between a grandchild and grandparents help children get to know their grandparents with less strain and full attention. That can also be restful for parents and give them some individual time with the remaining children.

Sharing of Skills and Interests

Sharing of skills, stories, interests, and travel are appropriate for grandparents and children. Oral histories make nice school projects for children, and they can use a cassette or videotape to make a permanent record for the future and for their own children. A grandparent may be able to take a grandchild on a special trip or visit, which will make the visit more enjoyable for both child and adult. Regular telephone communication keeps grandparents and grandchildren close. Cassette tapes, videos, and snapshots help grandparents share in children's growth.

Gift Giving

Although too many gifts can convert normal preschoolers to "gimme" children who never seem to have enough, special gifts in moderation are meaningful and memorable. Grandparents may want some parental guidance in gift selection to be sure you approve of their purchases. If you offer to help and give them a price range, you can guide them in selecting something you and your children will value.

Holidays and Traditions

Grandparents can be especially helpful in carrying out celebrations and holiday traditions that seem to be enhanced greatly by being shared. Although a few unpredictable and minor disasters often occur, your children will only remember the warmth and love—the tears, spilled liquids, and the occasional confrontations will be forgotten or remembered only with giggles.

If you have differences with your parents or in-laws that could cause unpleasant eruptions, you may wish to talk those through by telephone or in person beforehand. Everyone will have to make a few compromises, but it's best not to save the debate for the actual holiday celebration. It's important for your children to observe the love and respect in their family, although occasionally disagreements are normal and even provide learning experiences for your children.

Summary Advice

- Stay in touch with grandparents.
- Grandparents may be able to help.
- Don't take grandparent help for granted.
- Encourage shared learning.
- Communicate about gift giving.
- Families being together on holidays enhances relationships.

Maintaining Long-Distant Relationships with Grandchildren

I am a grandmother-to-be from Wisconsin. The problem is, my grandchild on the way lives in California. How can I create and maintain a relationship with my grandchild?

A visit or two a year will of course do much to help you feel close to your grandchildren, but that may not be possible, so consider the many alternatives. Videotapes can be helpful: the parents can document your grandchild's developmental milestones, such as turning over, crawling, sitting up, and walking. Even the "oohs" and "ahs" of a three-month-old baby are delightful to capture on videotape. If your children tape for themselves, perhaps a copy of those tapes will make a wonderful Grandparents Day gift for you.

As your grandchildren get a little older, weekly telephone calls can communicate closeness. At first, your grandchildren will only listen, but soon reports of their day and week will be shared. A good time to talk to them is a little while before bedtime. They seem to prefer most anything to sleep, so you can count on some pretty good communication to Grandmom.

Small gifts, cards, and brief letters can keep you in touch with them. If you ask them to send you their artwork, they and their parents will be glad to share their early scribblings. Save some of their drawings and their letters in a treasure box marked with their name. By the time they're teenagers, you'll have a collection that will please them and will also provide tangible evidence of your growing relationship.

If you or your grandchildren would rather not write, voice messages on cassette tapes can allow you to share stories. Record your response on their taped messages, and they can hear and remember what they said as well as your response. Cassette tapes are inexpensive enough so that you won't have to destroy them by recording over the original messages and those, too, can be kept to be listened to later.

School-age children often can fly to visit their grandparents for a week or two, giving them an excellent opportunity for independence and their parents a pleasant vacation without children. Be sure to share stories of your childhood with your grandchildren. That will make history a reality. Pass on your traditions and information about your interests. When they come to visit, teach them a favorite skill, whether it's needlepoint, fishing, or painting. By sharing your stories and skills, you will become closer despite the many miles separating you.

Parents "Adultizing" Daughter

I have a five-year-old granddaughter who gets too much attention. She is very attractive. Her parents are both over forty. Her father is a doctor, her mother has a Ph.D., and they consider themselves the experts. Recently, I received a picture of my granddaughter all made up with makeup; she looks like a made-up doll. Do you have a diplomatic suggestion to give to parents about sending the wrong messages?

If your granddaughter's makeup was the fun kind that children use when dressing up, I assume you wouldn't be concerned.

However, it sounds as if you are realistically worried about your children's emphasis on appearances and your granddaughter growing up too soon. These are well-grounded concerns.

Parents who overemphasize appearance, dressing up, and wearing makeup are conveying their value system to their children. Their children will try to live up to that value system and will constantly feel pressure to be admired for their beauty, their clothing, and their grown-up appearance. They may not learn that intelligence, perseverance, and kindness are better measures of living well. Furthermore, if adolescence doesn't provide these children with a sufficient number of admirers, they may feel ugly, unnoticed, inadequate, and even depressed.

Your own children, who have obviously achieved much intellectually, would not be happy if their daughter valued herself only for her surface beauty. They are, undoubtedly, so smitten by this miraculous child that they assume that their overpraise only builds their daughter's self-esteem. If you can possibly convey to them the message that indeed they will eventually be blamed by their daughter for the pressure to achieve such impossible goals she feels during her adolescence, they can use more moderate and realistic praise to build confidence without pressures. The rule of thumb I usually share with parents is that appropriate praise words should be chosen from parents' realistic values that children will be able to live up to; for example, *bright, good thinking, hardworking, kind, sensitive, responsible,* or *pretty.* Overpraise words like *gorgeous, brilliant, smartest,* and *genius,* when used regularly to compliment children, are impossible for any child to live up to and will cause adolescents continuous pressure and frustration.

Toddler Has Trouble Verbalizing

My eighteen-month-old grandson is very active and bright. He has a difficult time expressing himself, however. He will become frustrated when he points to something and it is not confirmed right away. How can we help him?

Your grandson is undoubtedly at the cutting edge of developing more vocabulary that will ease his frustration. As he points to an object he wants, give him the words for the object and ask him to repeat the word. When he does, praise his new use of the words as you grant him the object. If he can't quite say the word, repeat it again for him. Of course, any approximation to the word will be acceptable. When he whines and cries, ask him to use words and wait patiently for his delivery.

Reading and singing nursery rhymes to your grandson will also help him to expand his expressive vocabulary. You'll soon understand his special way of talking, which others who don't know him well will not yet understand. As you continue to be patient, your grandson's vocabulary will increase, and his frustration will decrease. By the "terrific" two's, you can expect a noticeable expansion in his verbal expression.

Grandchildren Lack Respect

We have several grandchildren. Here's my query: If the parents let things happen at home that are a very real source of irritation at our place, what do we do? My grandchildren are four and two. Their eating habits are atrocious, and our furniture is at stake. The two-year-old swishes food all over her high chair and holds her glass upside down. Mom and Dad don't even notice.

We went out for about an hour one Sunday and left our children with their children, and when we came back, "little one" was on our blue velveteen chair by the phone, peanut butter and jam sandwich "pieces" in her hand, in her hair, all over her face, neck, arms, and dress, and holding the phone. I held her at arms' length for my protection, sat her on the bathroom counter and washed her, and will have to admit, I was extremely irritated with her (or our son and his wife?). I washed her up but was fuming inside.

I don't want to cause a family problem. But how can we get across to our kids that we are protecting our well-earned furniture, walls, etc., because we are older and have already replaced our furniture and want these to last. Our children are good and loving parents, and we don't want to discourage them or put up a wall between us. It's "egg shells" almost every week.

Certainly your love for your children and grandchildren should not be destroyed by your very real need to protect your belongings. Those regular visits are worth preserving. Although it would be important for young children and grandchildren to learn respect for other's belongings, it's not worth destroying your relationship.

I would support using temporary "ugly" plastic cover-ups for velveteen chairs and special furniture for those grandchildren visits, and explain to all involved that you'll look forward to removing them when the children get better at following some simple house rules. Make the rules simple, and explain that they apply only to your home since Mom and Dad may prefer different ones for their own home. Your children will soon catch on. For special relief of the tension, you may wish to offer to come to their home on some Sundays where you won't have to worry about furniture.

If, underlying this whole furniture protection problem, you're hoping to change your children's child-raising style, you're taking on a more serious problem. Although I'm sure you know much about child rearing that your own children could learn from you, they need to be willing to ask for your help if your advice is to do any good. If they ask, don't hesitate to offer suggestions from your good experience. If they're not interested, permit them the freedom to raise their children on their own. Each generation has a right and responsibility to parent in its own way, and parenting in the 1990s offers special challenges and opportunities. Try to protect yourself from unnecessary stress and do enjoy your grandparenting.

Too Much Advice

I have a seven-month-old daughter, and my mother is driving me crazy. She says she's only giving me advice, but I can't seem to convince her that unless I ask for it, I really don't want her advice. Mom didn't do such a great job of rearing my brother and me. We have an alcoholic father, and Mother is very controlling. She's furious because I don't want my daughter around my father. He still drinks. I don't want my daughter around a nasty drunk. I especially don't want him holding her when he's been drinking. He was always very verbally abusive to us. My mother wants to make me feel guilty about this. I just want to be the kind of mother I always wanted, and that includes protecting my daughter from my father. Please help.

I certainly understand why you don't want your child around your father when he's had too much to drink. If you know of times when your father doesn't usually drink, you might take advantage of those opportunities to let your daughter and her grandfather get to know each other. When your dad is sober, you can also explain to him the reasons for your concern, if he'll listen. One always hopes that alcoholics will go for help.

When your mother gives you advice, you can say, "I'll take that into consideration." You certainly don't need to feel as if you have to follow her suggestions. Listen to her, take time to think about what she's said, but do what is best for you and your child.

25

Developing Your Own Parenting Style

From the moment of your child's birth to the time that child graduates from college, you will receive advice from well-meaning grandparents, aunts and uncles, friends, and teachers. Some of the advice will be helpful, and some will seem contradictory and outdated. Sorting out the advice and developing your own parenting style are especially difficult during your children's preschool years, when you may not have developed confidence in your own parenting style and when children are so unpredictable.

Read parenting books, listen to cassette tapes, watch videotapes, and consider how you were raised. Observe other parents and child-care professionals. Attending parenting classes for parents of preschoolers can also be helpful. Then develop confidence in your decisions that seem to work, and ask questions when they don't. Consider what is working for your children on a day-to-day basis, and think about the long-term values you have for your children. Discuss these with your children's other parent(s).

Unsolicited Advice

When others give you unsolicited advice, listen and indicate you'll think about the advice. You can even take notes to assure the advice-giving individuals that you will consider their recommendation. Sometimes the advice looks better after you've had time to think about it; sometimes it never looks good. It is important not to become defensive. The advice you tune out because you're annoyed at the advice giver may actually be helpful. Try to keep an open mind, but don't feel as though you must follow the advice if you don't like it. If the person continues to remind you of his or her good advice, say you've thought about it and appreciate the help, but you have a different approach you prefer. Let the person know you appreciate the support, and you hope he or she won't confuse the children by contradicting your or your spouse.

Building Confidence in Your Parenting

There are many correct approaches to parenting, and all parents make small mistakes while raising their children. You'll find your children are forgiving of your mistakes and won't even notice them. Children who feel loved by their parents are resilient enough to cope with these variables. If you find that some of the approaches you use aren't effective, ask others for advice and try their suggestions. If your children are having problems, go for professional help, but don't blame yourself for not taking other people's advice. Soon you'll discover which approaches are effective, and you will grow in confidence.

Whatever parenting style you select is likely to be criticized by your own children when they grow up. That seems to be part of normal development. If you're doing your best, your children will thrive, and you can feel good about the positive difference you make for them.

Summary Advice

- Read, listen, and observe.
- Ask questions when you have them.
- Respond that you'll think about it.
- Have confidence in yourself.

Sources

Abelson, P. H. *Preparing Children for the Future.* In *Science* 274 (13): 1819.

Carnegie Corporation of New York. *Years of Promise: A Comprehensive Learning Strategy for America's Children.* Executive summary. New York: Carnegie Task Force on Learning, 1996.

Rimm, S. B. *Why Bright Kids Get Poor Grades and What You Can Do About It.* New York: Crown Publishers, 1995.

———— *Dr. Sylvia Rimm's Smart Parenting.* New York: Crown Publishers, 1996.

———— "Sylvia Rimm on Raising Kids." Newspaper column. Los Angeles: Creators Syndicate.

Index